MW00632409

COLD HEARTS
WARM BODIES

The Secrets Inside Assisted Living

By

Jen Awinda

ISBN 978-1-958788-84-4 (Digital)

ISBN 978-1-958788-85-1 (Paperback)

ISBN 978-1-958788-86-8 (Hardcover)

Copyright © 2023 by Jen Awinda

All Rights Reserved. No part of this publication may be reproduced, distributed, or transmitted in any form or by any means, including photocopying, recording, or other electronic or mechanical methods without the prior written permission of the publisher. For permission requests, solicit the publisher via the address below.

Publify Publishing

1412 W. Ave B

Lampasas, TX 76550

publifypublishing@gmail.com

JenniferAwinda.com

CONTENTS

Foreword

"Grow old along with me! The best is yet to be, the last of life, for which the first was made. Our times are in his hand who saith, 'A whole I planned, youth shows but half; Trust God: See all, nor be afraid!"

- 'Robert Browning'

When we are young, we yearn for days to come. A child delights in birthdays and the next stage of life from entering kindergarten to learning to drive a car. The passing years are exciting, and expectations abound. The quote by Robert Browning is apt, yet few 'old people' truly believe in the premise of 'the best is yet to be...' With age comes unexpected challenges for many. Physical and/or cognitive decline highlight life for many who enter older age. Bodily functions begin to deteriorate and although humans have delayed the aging process in many ways due to scientific advances, better health care and nutrition, on the flip side, our longer lifespan has introduced pitfalls we could not have imagined 100 years ago. Families no longer live in the same regions together. Children move away and do not have close associations with grandparents or even their own parents. Adults work well into their 50's through their 80's and many may not be able to retire at all. Those that are lucky enough to retire may be financially compromised. The healthcare system is overwhelmed with the wave of Baby Boomers entering their retirement years. Chronic conditions, diseases, and dementia is prevalent, and seems to be creeping into younger age groups. Environmental factors have changed the fabric of food nutrition and living conditions. And stress has entered every facet of life. As we look at aging, the hurdles seem to only get higher.

"By the time you're eighty years old, you've learned everything. You only have to remember it."

- George Burns

Jen Awinda, author of Cold Hearts Warm Bodies, takes us on a journey into a facet of aging that has been whispered about and hidden in the fabric of the modern senior living communities. The model of 'Assisted Living' being marketed in the U.S. today is that of a safe place to receive compassionate care in a community that specializes in providing professional 24-hour assistance, social interaction and chef prepared, nutritious meals. For those that can afford $3,000 to $10,000 or more a month, these communities roll out the red carpet, offering personal care services in a setting that may look more like a five-star hotel from the outside. Unlike a hospital, many of these communities have bistros, libraries, theaters, gyms that rival any fitness center, sweeping staircases in the lobby, beautiful artwork hanging on the walls, and nurses and caregivers attending to the needs of the residents, most of the time. Jennifer takes us behind the walls, into the complex daily workings of these senior living communities.

As an executive director (E.D.), Jen is responsible for the daily operations of her communities. In her book, Ms. Awinda details the unassigned work that may fall to the E.D. such as, the countless times a caregiver calls off in the middle of the night – leaving no staff on duty, lawsuits brought by families who do not understand the scope of responsibilities within an assisted living, investigating missing opioids in medication carts, or homeless people living in vacant rooms. Years in the making, Cold Hearts Warm Bodies chronicles some of Jen's experiences working in senior living. Through multiple states, in numerous communities, under different titles and for several different companies, she provides a picture that is both poignant and horrific. Yes, it is meant to shock and shine a light on an industry that needs shoring up. Those who work in this industry serve a forgotten population of aging adults with limited physical and mental abilities and are caught in this system. Some may turn away from the cover, yet we are the caregivers of these vulnerable individuals and some day you, dear reader, may need the assistance of one of these corporations.

"I'm a strong person," says Jen. "I feel I can handle anything. But to see these residents being neglected day after day, decade after decade, and caregivers just walk off the job leaving residents alone, it's not ok. I can't just keep turning my eyes and collecting paychecks like too many people keep doing out of survival mode. If we don't have staffing or the tools required to care for residents, how can we advertise compassionate care?"

Jen knows and works with numerous people who do care and have dedicated their lives to helping people in the healthcare setting. Like her, there are individuals who go to work each day to bring a positive light to the industry. There are places that are not 'The Ghost Town in the Dusty Desert' or 'Heaven Forbid Senior Living' (fictitious names for real assisted living facilities featured in this book). Unfortunately, the locations that provide good care are outnumbered by those that put profits over people. And many health care facilities across the country are at the mercy of employees who may or may not show up to work and perform their job, in a time when the nation struggles to find workers. "We are gasping for air in the senior tsunami and we're barely feeling the first wave of Baby Boomers with younger people from Generation X filtering in too."

- Jen Awinda.

Educating families on how to partner with their community, and the questions to ask before stepping into a community is important. Government oversight and regulations are set in place to protect a patient or resident and yet many times they are overlooked or, due to need, they are under-reported. "Healthcare is broken", a statement heard throughout the U.S. every day. But what is being done?

"When I started writing this book, I asked over 40 colleagues for stories. Out of fear of being blacklisted or 'cancelled' many were scared to participate or had signed something by their previous company dictating they weren't allowed to talk about their separation. All but one person that did participate asked to remain Anonymous and that's because he retired a few years ago. We desperately need people to discuss and recognize the problems so we can find a way forward. Our parents today, you and I tomorrow." - Jen Awinda. This is Jen's way of shining light on the senior living state of emergency that the people who control this industry don't want to talk about, by telling her story, dozens of stories from her colleagues, and the story of hundreds, maybe thousands, of healthcare workers.

Foreword By: Diva Givens

Senior Living Executive & Dementia Practitioner

CHAPTER ONE

Frisky Business

It must have been around 10 years ago that a colleague of mine said, "You've got to watch the PBS documentary but be forewarned, it's going to hit close to home." 'Life and Death in Assisted Living' uncovered horrifying stories of resident neglect, bed sores, and a confused retired NFL player that died after mistaking a bottle of bleach for drinking water. It laid the case for facilities that admitted people beyond their scope of practice. The stories were worst-case scenarios since not all assisted livings are negligent to the extent of residents ingesting poison. Managers work to the brink of exhaustion to do what's right by families, employees, the big bosses, and the should-be movie stars we care for 24 hours per day with special celebrations on holidays. Unfortunately, not everyone does what's right by other people, or cares about the often-provocative seniors that are hidden away in assisted living communities.

Many residents are quite the character with absolutely no filters on their mouths, especially when they feel helpless or depressed, or after developing dementia. For decades senior living professionals, like myself, have tried relentlessly to eliminate the stigma about assisted livings not being nursing homes. We have made wonderful relationships with residents and families, often educating them on services that assisted living can and cannot provide differentiating from the services offered in skilled nursing and rehab facilities. Over the past few years, the demographic of residents moving into assisted living has changed from people with limited mobility to residents that are completely dependent on care. We admit high-acuity residents just to keep the census up, all the while not having committed staff to care for them. Many of my colleagues are in the same situation, swept up in a tsunami of complaints and complacency. I'd be upset too if my mother wasn't receiving the care services promised at the time of move in. Many complaints are justifiable especially when you're paying upward of $5,000.00 and $10,000.00 per month.

Working in senior living for so long I have seen lots of interesting things and been put in some precarious situations. As an executive director I have witnessed and reported abuse and neglect and have had to initiate hard conversations with families, visitors, employees, and residents. I have had to call Adult Protective Services on family members. I had to ban people from visiting their loved ones. I have had to walk-out terminated employees securing company equipment and name badges. I have evicted residents and even called the police on the ones that committed illegal acts and threatened other residents' lives. Involving law enforcement gets tricky when mental health problems and dementia is involved but we're talking guns and knives and illegal drugs in some cases. Most issues don't call for authorities and are most often residents with their drama, indifference by staff, and families not always on their best behavior.

Working in assisted living provides the opportunity to meet all sorts of people from all walks of life. I'm surprised I didn't get to meet one of the real Golden Girls. The innovators and move makers of time before are the vulnerable senior population in need of care today. The famous ones you may have heard of but mostly the unfamous people who raised the most of us. They really did travel down the road and back again. They led full, adventurous, and sometimes promiscuous lives only to be hidden away in their last days with caregivers attending to their every stage. Those once strong and independent are now senior living residents some of whom no longer recognize danger and are often cared for by the negligent.

I did meet several influencers over the years, and I even got to work with one of Frank Sinatra's girls who wrote and published her memoirs. She still lives in the assisted living community I managed a couple of years ago. I worked with a rocket scientist who was brilliant, but her memories were dissolved by dementia. I have worked with lots of doctors, nurses, teachers, and WW2 parachute packers. One of the hardest situations to witness was that of a Holocaust survivor with dementia who relived terrifying memories during the sun-downing and over-night hours. She reverted to speaking Polish and forgot all about English. She spoke French, too. I remember her telling me that she was from Poland and when she fled the war in her country, she had to cross multiple check points that had armed soldiers. She carried with her a piece of paper with words written in a language the soldiers couldn't read and they let her through the check points thinking it was a legitimate pass since she showed confidence. She said one time a soldier had the paper upside down acting like he understood what he was reading.

In the early 2000's I worked with one of the girlfriends of the prohibition gangster, Al Capone. Everyone could tell she used to be a show girl, and a frisky one at that. I will always remember her, especially because she shared the same name as my little sister. She was 95 years old and just as much a hoochie-coochie girl as she had been back in the days. She was proud to be a freak. Once in the dining room during a valentine's day party, the executive director at the time was a young, handsome British man who had no idea what was about to happen to him. As he sat in a chair watching the karaoke entertainment, miss 95-year-old hoochie-coochie lady caught him unaware and began giving him a stripper style lap-dance. She was all over him and he couldn't push her away too hard or stand up to run fearing he might knock her over. The executive director was blushing beet red, uncomfortable, and trying every which way to get out of the embarrassing predicament. It was so inappropriate. Hoochie-Coochie stood in front of him straddled with a foot beside his hip while she gyrated and grunted pushing her cleavage in his face. He almost had a heart attack. That was probably the longest 60 seconds of his life.

At Halloween that same sweet and innocent-looking little old lady with the short white curly hair did a number on a couple of fathers who brought their children in for trick-or-treating. Any resident that wanted the children to come for candy decorated their front doors down a long hallway. Costumed children ran up and down the halls between 6PM and 7PM while their slower parents straggled behind trying to keep an eye on them. I led the children and tried to keep them corralled but children have no control of where their legs go when they see bowls of candy waiting for them in multiple doorways. Costumed kids were everywhere.

There were a lot of people that year and I had no volunteers. I was also trying to make sure other residents were not disturbed. Then I noticed a father walking away from Miss Hoochie-Coochie's apartment laughing with eyes WIDE opened which made me wonder what the heck had just happened. I went to the room and a different father was trying desperately to get out of her clutches. She tried to sexually assault the poor guy. He didn't bring his kids back for Easter or Halloween ever again. Miss Hoochie-Coochie goosed the maintenance man several times and had repeated sexual encounters in the hallways with a resident that never got off his red electric scooter. They would fondle one another right there by the elevator on the second floor eventually disappearing into a room that wasn't always one of theirs.

There are always interesting residents moving in and dramatic events going on in assisted living. It doesn't matter if the residents have dementia or not. And it doesn't matter if the residents are bed bound or not. Soap-Opera-drama finds a way and we must remind workers to be careful when taking pictures and videos of the residents. "Don't post things on social media or capture incriminating things on your cell phones." Everyone has their devices close to their hearts. The addiction to technology or whatever is taking away the attention of the workers makes me really concerned for the future. I, myself, rely heavily on my phone for both business and pleasure but not to steal company time and ignore the residents. Whether they'll admit it or not, even the best executive directors and administrators are in a constant battle to prevent neglect knowing workers aren't paying enough attention.

We're all trying to remain in compliance with state regulations and keep corporate invisibles, employees, and customers happy. That's a challenge knowing we all have witnessed employees hiding away from the residents, starring at their cell phones, gossiping in groups, workers on the clock but socializing like they're not. We depend on workers to care for our high acuity residents yet continue to witness too many not paying attention, not engaging residents, and hiding in rooms to avoid helping residents. We witness workers not being supported by supervisors, and often not willing to report concerns. We witness workers not being recognized by the out-of-touch invisibles that generate policies and reports from afar. We witness workers not being treated with respect by families and residents that scream. And we witness executive directors and staffing-agencies covering shifts when employees don't show up, that is if managers don't simply turn their eyes to residents going without care and employees working alone. I have known several managers that broke down and cried because the stress was so overwhelming.

Anonymous Story # 1.

———◆———

"I was dumb enough to be corporate human resources (HR), craziest crap I have ever done. One night the executive director called and said I am sick I am so sick. I said go to the doctor. Caregivers had been putting Ex-Lax in her coffee at least twice a day for months. Then when she was sick, they broke into her office took all the HR files and put them in a burn barrel in the courtyard and burned them."

Working in assisted living will test even the most patient people. We deal with verbal and physical aggression towards us, hitting, punching, kicking, biting, and residents and families bullying and screaming at us, even spitting at us. While some elders in assisted living have wonderful dispositions with interesting stories and secrets that they're desperate to share with anyone who will listen, many facilities take care of people that are in terrible pain with snappy attitudes who are mad at the world. The residents require a lot of intimate care services, and many are completely dependent on us for everything including spoon and tube feeding. With acuity levels so high it's challenging for facilities lacking systems such as communication and training for staff to care for people with advanced dementia and medical needs. Sadly, too many locations are mismanaged and infested with bugs, thugs, and drugs, specifically some of the facilities in low-income areas subsidized by state Medicaid.

I have worked at different locations with residents stealing, consuming, and selling drugs, and even one guy losing crystal meth in his laundry hamper. Our suspicions were validated when it was found by housekeeping. Trying to change the culture with acquisitions or become the new executive director of facilities in crisis is a challenge that would make anyone question their choice of employment. My colleagues and I encountered homeless squatters in vacant rooms, and even residents prostituting themselves to cover their bills and habits. One friend told me of a resident cooking crystal meth in his apartment...cooking meth in assisted living...! I thought the guy on heroine that invited homeless drug-addicts to shower in his apartment was bad. Those facilities are very hard to get on track because it means sacrificing revenue by kicking out the troublemakers while the sales director of the quarter grovels for new admissions.

Senior living has taught me all sorts of things from how to get rid of bedbugs, to understanding what it means to 'hit' or 'blaze' the dab-pen; Bring in the bedbug sniffing dogs, and a dab pen is a vape-pen for smoking cannabis wax or extract. I found that 'blazing the dab pen' is very popular with most people living and working at Heaven Forbid Senior Living, a facility I once managed and will elaborate on later.

Anonymous Story # 2

——◆——

"*Drugs, including heroin and marijuana. In one case we knew which resident the drugs belonged to. Another time it was crystal meth that we found but since the resident was bed bound, we knew it was their family that brought it in. Another drug of choice was opioids and Xanax off the street that were not part of the resident's medication list. There was a visitor that came in and out pretty often. The pills were in a container which was found by one of the caregivers."*

Anonymous Story # 3

"A woman moved in that had previously been homeless, but she brought in some of her friends. So other residents felt unsafe with the stranger friends. A fight ensued between her and another resident. We eventually had to kick her out because there was constant coming and going and we didn't know if it was drug related. There was a knife drawn and we called the police."

4

"I'm prepping and I got like five flies buzzing around the food. There were so many flies in the kitchen, and I remember one day a coworker got a long broom to get underneath the metal rack and he pulled out a bunch of trash from under there and there were maggots in the trash. And the residents be complaining about the flies all the time."

5

"Nobody be working. Everyone be taking smoke breaks. Just sitting around texting and playing on their phones, blazing the dab pen. Anybody got a dab pen? One resident asked so I gave it to him, and he started hitting it in the dining room. Ain't nobody gonna talk to you, nobody enforces the laws. I vape everywhere. But I hit my dab pen outside. Residents and employees be buying weed from each other. One girl was going to the dispensary for a resident. Nobody be cleaning. That's why we have so many roaches crawling everywhere. One server was about to get fired so she quit and then they made her a caregiver."

Regardless of the pestilence or drama in facilities, they are still businesses that need new customers because people move out and pass-away. Sales must always be the number one focus, at least that's how corporate offices make us feel. We've got to generate revenue. We can't have jobs if we don't have residents. But we can't have residents if we don't have caregivers. Where are the caregivers anyways? The revolving door never seems to stop. No one ever knows who will be the next to give notice or be escorted out as a trespasser. Or get so frustrated they walk off the job. Sometimes they abandon their jobs in groups leaving no one to work in that department. Or like an incident that happened; a caregiver went buck-wild, took off her scrub top and threw it at the executive director. Then in her bra she ran down the halls and outside around the building yelling and carrying on while being chased by management and finally subdued by a police officer she ended up biting. We could only presume she was high on drugs. Many times, caregivers are simply 'no call no shows." Ghosts! And that's not to mention the frustration encountered by managers, cooks, or any of the other members of staff.

No one wants to talk about it, but we've got nationwide problems to address as a society regarding how to care for our elders. Medicare wasn't designed with the anticipation of seniors living well into their 90s and 100s. It appears unsustainable along with Medicaid and Social Security which is what many seniors rely on to barely scrape by. Too many elders already skip meals and medications because they cannot afford them. There are reasons why the suicide rate of seniors is so high and it's a direct reflection of how we treat our aging population. Families don't have the time, energy, skills, or patience to stay home caring for their loved ones since so many adult children must work well beyond retirement age just to eat. Our elders live their entire lives contributing to society and when they become dependent on care they are forgotten about and thrown away in the end. To quote a dear friend of mine, "We can put the old folks in a closet out of sight and let them rot there, or we can treat them as we ourselves would – and one day will – wish to be treated." No one wants to grow old, at least not in our country.

How long is too long to wait to urinate, before a person who can still tell you they've got to go can no longer hold their bladder resulting in the need for another protective undergarment, clean set of clothes, and potentially fresh set of bed linens? We are here for the residents, but why must they lay in soiled briefs and urine-soaked sheets up to their necks all night? Not everyone is willing to provide intimate personal care services so there is always a need for caregivers. When caregivers are asked, 'why do you work in assisted living' their response is "I'm here for the residents." Yet, it's an oxymoron when residents press their call-buttons, and no one comes for half an hour or longer. And that was the norm before the staffing shortage was worsened by the COVID-19 pandemic.

6

"Caregivers are so unprofessional, two of them were talking about strippers and twerking in front of the residents. Another caregiver convinced families that she's the only competent person and she makes med errors all the time. We are always hiring, always always hiring. One person showed up to an interview in booty shorts and a tank top and slippers with rhinestones on em'. And the new caregiver that already started orientation the other day never came back and she ain't answering her phone but that happens all the time. They usually don't show up on the first day."

There's a constant influx of new caregivers and personalities, often wonderful people but sometimes abusive and cold-hearted. Everyone is sweet during the interview or pre-admission assessment. Who we really get comes out around a week or so after hire or move-in. And scheduling is a fluid nightmare with all the caregivers coming and going and not showing up to work and needing time off and wanting their schedules changed. The inside joke amongst some of my colleagues and me is, "caregivers must be independently wealthy because they sure do take a lot of time off." When they show up to work, they disregard the rules like leaving residents' narcotics on bedside and dining room tables, and pre-pouring all the residents' medications to save time so they can spend more sitting around.

Staff sign off indicating they've completed tasks, yet blatantly falsify documents. It's not just caregivers doing shady work because some managers and regionals call unethical shots even preying on residents. A caregiver signed off indicating having given medications to the 90-year-old veteran who was left in the sweltering transport van all afternoon, all evening, all night, until he was found dead the following day. Negligence is over the top and falsifying documents has become systematic with corporate leaders and managers simply looking the other way, often doing shameless and illegal acts then blaming it on a single employee to cover their butts and the company. There are some shady people working in senior living.

7

"*I had to be the interim executive director and there was a retired colonel that had tons of money, and the Vice President of Operations (VPO) came to assist, kind of got friendly with this elderly guy. All of a sudden, they're in a sexual relationship together, the VPO and an Elderly resident. I called the Senior Vice President (SVP) and said do you realize the VPO is in a relationship with a resident? He was like, she's just overly friendly. The resident's kids couldn't believe what was happening. I mean what are they going to do? She moved him to Montana, married him, he died, and she wasn't married to him long enough to get his pension, so she shipped his ashes to his daughter in a cardboard box.*"

During the day it's evident some employees would rather make friends with one another than take care of the residents. They hang out together, forcing managers to schedule breaks. "Uh, everyone can't leave on break at once. Remember, we are here for the residents." There usually aren't enough workers on the floor anyways so how can multiple people leave at once? Conversing employees congregate out of sight while the resident's garbage hasn't been taken out, resident's laundry hasn't been done in weeks and much of it goes missing when it does get done. Folding the laundry before it gets wrinkled and putting it away is asking for a lot when some executive directors now must give bonuses to their employees just to come in to work their scheduled shift.

Sales are at the top, and housekeeping is at the bottom of the 'priorities' list according to all the industry partners asked and interviewed. Regular weekly housekeeping is practically non-existent for most. Residents that receive housekeeping may be better off without if it's by untrained staff that uses muddied mop water and funky-stained rags. Common sense doesn't grow in every garden. Training housekeepers and sanitizing properly wasn't even considered before COVID-19 prompted infection control policies to be followed for a few weeks here and there, even though C-diff and influenza were common prior to 2020. C-Diff, short for Clostridioides Difficile, is a bacteria that inflames the colon causing diarrhea. Most seniors in assisted living have medical issues and tend to be dehydrated so having diarrhea can lead to serious complications. C-diff is contagious so sanitizing commonly touched surfaces is extremely important to prevent all sorts of unwanted illness. Post pandemic, people still aren't taking sanitizing seriously.

8

"I was the new executive director and the housekeeper that had been working there for years wanted to impress me with how well she cleans rooms. She asked me to come see a vacant room that was staged with furniture. Right when I walked in, I could see the dirt and trash under the bed. She walked over to the window to show me how clear the glass was, but my eyes were drawn to the window seal that had dead flies and dirt caked in the spaces of the metal. I pointed out the debris, then walked over to the

refrigerator which probably hadn't been cleaned ever. The bathroom still had an almost empty tube of toothpaste, an old balled up tissue and other garbage in the medicine cabinet. Being polite I played it off as - in all those years she'd been working there she was never given a checklist of things to look for. In my mind I was like, "come on, really?"

When there's down time workers tend to refrain from going the extra mile like sanitizing anything or simply engaging residents in fun activities. If we're here for the residents, then why hide or stand in the med room? Even when caregivers see the residents are bored or anxious without anything to do, they still aren't interested in initiating any relief for the residents. It's no secret many residents feel lost in a foreign place, and they're bored to tears perpetuating feelings of hopelessness and depression. Stand-offish workers do not offer any hope, yet we're supposed to give 'please show up to work' bonuses to warm bodies with cold hearts that would rather stare at social media than share meaningful moments with evidently lonely seniors. In all my years there has only been a handful of workers that took the initiative to regularly engage the residents in the final years of life. They're often the same caregivers who carry the weight of others that call-off. They keep turning over because they do all the work while the lazy workers are retained as warm bodies out of desperation due to staffing shortages. The lack of care instigates pressure-ulcers, and potential litigation seems to always be lurking.

Executive directors keep turning over feeling defeated and often sabotaged. Marketers continue turning over often feeling guilty for over promising care while feeling beaten up over net growth and census. There is only so much we can do when there are not enough people who are physically willing to get their hands dirty and do the hard work of caregiving. Real caregiving consists of smells and bodily fluids, changing soiled adult briefs, emptying catheter and ostomy bags, giving hands on showers, dressing, grooming, transferring, and other intimate personal care services.

Caregivers that care are sleep deprived and overwhelmed, rushing from one resident to the next because residents are on the same wake, eat, toileting and sleep cycle. They were exhausted before the pandemic, but the fatigue from the aftermath of pulling double shifts just to afford to pay rent, eat and have enough gas money to get to work is really getting to people. Frontline employees are supposedly appreciated by corporate yet lucky to receive a $25 gift card for Christmas, or a turkey at Thanksgiving while corporate high earners have no problems taking a week or two off here and there on top of big-dollar bonuses.

9

"I was the office manager and every year around the middle of October the executive director had me create a fund-raising flyer to send with the monthly statements to families. The flyer was for collecting donations for caregiver Christmas bonuses. We did it for years before a new company took over. A little over $12,000 was raised intended to be split between the few-dozen caregivers. But the new corporate office took the money and handed out holiday turkeys to everyone instead."

Care services are not commonly provided by generously paid corporate executives. Most of them are strictly virtual 'paper people' that won't step foot in the facility to fill a shift or change an adult diaper. They're totally oblivious to the real care needs of their revenue source, which only adds to caregiver's complacency and resentment for having to do all the hard work of caring for the residents at low wages. I have worked for two companies where my corporate leaders stepped in to cook, provide personal care services, and assist with maintenance. Good companies that care are rare. Thankfully there are still a few of them out there. But don't expect much from corporate big-wigs and neither may have a budget for holiday turkeys.

Several years into the pandemic the entire country sees there aren't enough people willing to work across the nation. This is nothing new in assisted living because we've been dealing with the staffing shortage for over a decade. Still companies are building and acquiring more senior living properties... with their lawyers on standby knowing it's only a matter of time before they'll be needed to dispute lawsuits. Yes, often a result of negligence, but sometimes the lawsuits are just crazy families looking for a check. Boots on the ground feel it every day while corporate invisibles create new senior living facilities and management companies without taking seriously the question of who will provide hands on care?

10

"All the managers got sick, all on the same day. Right at Christmas time so my nurse tried to do everything. I was not capable of doing everyone's jobs for two weeks. And corporate was not there to help. They wouldn't even send someone from the corporate office to answer phones. The corporate guy said, "you sound frustrated" and I said because I am frustrated and I have all these requirements of the nursing and charting and we are not going to be able to meet all of those, this cannot be business as usual, and when you see something isn't signed off - too bad, you can either come here and do this job in the community or it's not

happening. And that burnt out all of us. We all got kind of a disgruntled feeling of what kind of support we got."

11

"The corporate office worked remotely during COVID, and they wouldn't come into the building. They weren't worried about my health; they were worried about what was going on in the community. They said, well we can't go in, there's covid in your building, but I could go in every day. They were scared of getting sick, but our caregivers were scared too."

It seems every year there are dozens of 'assisted living grand openings' in the United States. And that has nothing to do with the excess of senior living management companies popping up, most of which prioritize profits while ignoring red flags. Do they even know or care about the red flags? Or do they just add to their portfolio and 'pay the fines? Many 'invisibles' don't know what is in their own policies and procedures manuals, or what is required to be in-compliance with state regulations. I personally haven't seen them volunteering to fill open caregiving shifts in communities even though that's what pays the bills. It seemed most invisibles wouldn't step foot near the building during the pandemic because they didn't want to risk getting sick. But they sure did expect caregivers, and managers to be in the facility. And most importantly they expected the marketers to net growth, continue pounding the concrete and selling rooms.

12

"Corporate acts like they care, may even pop in a few times a year, but it's all a front. All they care about is their bonus."

13

"When I first started at one community everyone was scared of the VP coming, and he liked me because the building was clean and he liked that, but he would come through and see the popcorn popper and say something like, how old is that popcorn in there, and I said it is popped fresh every day. Then he said you know there's a lightbulb burned out. Why do you have to do that? And that's why so many of us are leaving this industry. None of my residents are dying of stale popcorn. If I walk through your house right now is everything perfect? I take pride in running this building and you can see we're doing our best."

14

"I was at a Superbowl party, and it was half time, and the phone rings and it's Dick Nibbler saying, 'well good it's halftime and I've got to go over these numbers with you'. like this couldn't wait until Monday morning. And that's what drove me away from that company. The ED at a sister property, she and I had all these codes. *She'd text saying, 'the eagle has landed', and that meant corporate was in, and when they'd leave my community, I would text, "Elvis has left the building." That was the fun, that support from just being able to vent and she even started calling him Mr. Nibbler."*

We're all pushing for 100% census knowing a brand-new marketing director may be fired if they don't net growth each month. All the while invisibles take a week off here and there for personal getaways. There's a limited budget for training the frontline employees that physically take care of their revenue source, the residents. Marketing budgets are much higher than the budgets for resident's quality of life activities especially when you factor in the 'corporate meetings' for training their salespeople. For that there must be travel expenses, hotel accommodations, food, and other costly details. Having well trained Sales and Marketing Directors is necessary to find new potential residents and "Move them in! Appropriate or not!" But the activities budget is a joke.

Problems arise when residents don't have fun things to do after move-in, complicated by lack of training and care, and disappointment with the food. But some assisted livings don't put any love into the meals to the extent of serving slop that my spoiled dog wouldn't eat. Much of the food is processed and the several-week cycle menu consists of the same old worn-out recipes of chicken, beef and pork, chicken, beef, and pork, with a Friday fish fry, day in and out, week after week, leading to more complaints. And you know most dietary staff members aren't interested in food presentation. It seems like only a handful of locations don't slop it on the plate and serve it up luke-warm.

Activities seem to be monotonous if they happen at all, and housekeeping slips here and there. The executive director has budgeting, licensing, and other business pressures so there's limited time for attention to detail while we have 100 residents, plus each of their families, all wanting a few minutes of the nurse or executive director's time. And of course, every hospice and home health representative desperate for patients want time too. There's so much room for error, and some families have no patience or regard for how hard all of this is for the facility employees. Some even verbally and sexually harass caregivers making them want to quit.

15

———◆———

"One husband who didn't live in the community would come and visit his wife who lived on the second floor. He would start having sex with his wife, then press the emergency call button to call caregivers. He just wanted us to watch, and we did not want to see two old people having sex."

We're helping your loved-one and you yell and disrespect us. We're redirecting inappropriate behaviors and overseeing the personal care services of dozens of people, trying to get everyone dressed, and fed on time, have showers and clean linens, have their apartments cleaned and fun things to do throughout the day, and we get yelled at. Even the brand-new facilities that do a wonderful job at providing care, and there most certainly are many of them, they can't do a good enough job according to some families and residents. They're paying all that money, expecting much more than is legally permitted in assisted living, and sometimes expecting more than is humanly possible when there are only a few caregivers to 50 or more incontinent residents with dementia. No matter how hard we try, we can't do anything right according to some families. Managers and employees arguing and saying incriminating things doesn't help alleviate the frustration. Screaming at staff, scolding, waving their fingers in worker's faces, and even some predators that start sexual relationships with employees, not because they fell in-love. A dietary manager and a server broke the hand washing sink in the kitchen. Why did they think that little sink could hold a 150-pound woman under pressure?

16

"The nurse developed an intimate relationship with a caregiver, and they were taking inappropriate pictures together. They made it well known and there was favoritism going on and the corporate office didn't do anything."

17

"I was Human Resources, and I got a call at midnight from the executive director. The caregiver was sleeping with a very elderly man, and he was paying her money. The caregiver didn't think there was anything wrong with it because he needed the attention, and she needed the money for her bills. "No, I love him, he's just the sweetest guy and he offered to give me money. And we're all good with it, what's the big deal?" And I was like Are You Kidding Me!"

I once worked as an office manager in a dementia care community, the new executive director was thrown into what she coined as "bugs, thugs and drugs." On her first day she had to deal with bed bugs and exterminators. On her second day her life was threatened by an employee she fired for harassing another member of staff. On her third day she showed up toting a 9mm in a new gun-purse that her husband ran out and bought for her. From caregivers slashing each other's tires in the parking lot, to residents whipping it out in the dining room, I'm not joking when I say assisted living is Golden Girl Drama All Day!

18

————◆————

"A bed alarm was going off, and since there weren't any caregivers in sight, I went to the room to check on the resident. I did a quick double knock, opened the door slightly, announced myself and noticed movement towards the bottom of the bed. I entered the room and saw clothes and a used adult diaper on the floor. But I paid it no mind knowing quite a few residents with dementia tend to take off their briefs and clothes. I walked into the room a bit further and saw the resident in bed straddled and gyrating on top of another half-naked resident. I turned and bolted out of the room embarrassed for walking in on them. They were both consenting adults so the only thing I could do was call and inform both families of the romance that had been kindled."

This kind of thing happens often in facilities, and over the years I have witnessed things that make a little romance no big deal. Just about every location I've ever been in has captivating reality show grade drama and a revolving door of employees that do and say things they think are funny but could be used against them in a court of law. We all experience a fair share of workers saying, 'that isn't my job' and 'we've always done it this way' and know of people who could make a change for the better but choose to collect their bi-weekly pay and look the other way.

Even in challenged facilities family members and visiting friends catch snippets of tension while somewhere deep inside they know, "my loved-one is better cared for here than at my house because I cannot deal with it." And most of the time they're right, they need help. Last night one resident with dementia who gets agitated and emotional in the evening (commonly known as 'Sundowning') got upset with me and everyone else. She kept asking, "Where is the Theater?" We only have the one large T.V. on the other side of the wall and that was not sufficient. She cussed me out saying she went to the theater last night, pointing and saying that's the door she went out (the side door), and we're trying to trap her inside the building, and she's going to call the police, and on she went. Then she was confused about her medications saying I don't take this, and I don't take that. I thought she was going to throw her pills or her water cup at me or do something else so I could not turn my back on her.

19

"We offer 24-hour care, but staffing is a problem. We don't have someone at their beckon call, even in the daytime when management are there. When you have communities that have 50, 60, 70, 80 people with dementia, how are caregivers truly able to be that attentive versus one-on-one care."

20

"*I run a support group for families to address their challenges and experiences with dementia. I offer educational and practical knowledge. Last week I hosted a support group on expectations because there is a family moving their loved one out because the call light wasn't answered within two minutes. It was answered, but like ten minutes later. We try to educate the families that we don't have one caregiver dedicated to one resident. If they were at home the family may be able to respond instantaneously but it's not realistic in a community with dozens upon dozens of residents with two or three caregivers working, or even four caregivers working if you can staff that well. We let them know during the discovery process when the marketer initially begins working with the family, we discuss expectations. Whether the family hears and understands that or not is another story. We are a community, and we are not going to be able to care for your loved one the way a family would, and even some families are unable to do that.*"

People fall all the time. There are fall prevention trainings but all we can really do is move obstacles and remind people to use their walkers. But they forget all the time. Some of them sit in wheelchairs all day losing strength in their legs and they try to stand up and they fall but they're not eligible for physical therapy unless they get really hurt. A lot of the people on Hospice can't get physical therapy because they would have to pay privately for it. Every resident is a severe fall risk, and some people fall repeatedly. And the ones who qualify for physical therapy don't want to do it, so they keep falling. The families get all angry at us like it's our fault for not being by every resident's side at every moment of every day. We try our best but there's only so much we can do. The unrealistic expectations of some families who don't understand the aging process, the decline of dementia, and the dying process has us constantly worried about potential lawsuits.

No matter how much we love our family member, when confusion sets in and they start yelling and lashing out for what appears to be no reason, not really making sense but trying to convince you they know what they're talking about, and when they start becoming violent, it's time to consider moving them into a senior care community. The lady looking for the theater cannot recognize danger, and she cannot be left alone. But her family thinks she's only 'a little confused sometimes' because they don't spend enough time with her to see she's advanced in her dementia. Daily phone calls and weekly visits doesn't provide a clear picture. Had the side-door been unlocked that night she would have gone right outside not knowing where she was and unable to consider the consequences. She's awake most of the night going in and out of rooms, wandering all around the memory care unit opening cabinets and handling anything her curious mind finds interesting. Let's be realistic, we don't have enough staff to follow her around all night long, and every other wandering resident while also ensuring residents in their beds are dry. She, and residents like her, is the reason we must lock-up all chemicals and lock-away tools and sharp objects she could hurt herself or someone else with. She could mistake bleach for drinking water. It takes a lot of energy and staff members to take care for her and for the many other residents like her.

CHAPTER TWO

Choice Steak and Lobster

Assisted living is much different than the visions of sweet ole' elders singing, "You Are My Sunshine," and playing Bingo. Yes, they still play Bingo. Yet, many often discount it's a bunch of grownups looking forward to orgasms be they obtained behind closed doors or in common areas. Some seniors may have forgotten a few things, they may even have advanced dementia. But they are still adults, and they haven't forgotten about sex. Sex and Love are forever even if there had been a disinterest before.

You don't need to enter a resident's private room to see things you wish you hadn't because activities are happening all day and I'm not referring to what's posted on a calendar. It's common to see residents with dementia walking down the hall naked or half dressed. From time to time a male resident will whip it out in a common area, like the dining room, and begin masturbating in front of everyone not necessarily understanding, or perhaps not caring, that he's in the wrong place for that. There are many relationships developed amongst the residents who still want to be loved and held romantically like the rest of us. The hard part is trying to decipher if someone is being manipulated or bullied in some way.

Recently I was almost called into arbitration regarding a family member suing a dementia-care facility because their mom was caught giving a blowjob to another resident in a room. The female resident was very friendly and social but for some reason the family assumes their mother would never want to touch a man again just because she has advanced dementia. If she wasn't forced or coerced or upset or trying to get away, and there weren't any falls or fractures or broken skulls, how does it justify paying the family money?

Sometimes residents with dementia, as do people in general, behave like teenagers in puppy-love cuddling on the couch. But even teenager's experiment. And sometimes when there's only one or two male residents and there are a dozen women wanting to feel loved, the residents in the facility are down with O.P.P. (Other People's Property). They're adults who don't have to worry about pregnancy and are living their lives like it's Golden! It's no secret there are high STD rates in senior-housing neighborhoods. Thankfully it's not as high when residents live in a small facility group. In assisted living all we can do is encourage residents to do it behind closed doors, document and notify the family and physician. Is it a pattern? Not necessarily but quite possibly.

21

"From time to time we see a resident walking down the hallway naked in memory care. It's just part of the disease process so we're all used to that. What's difficult is when the confused resident believes another resident, or a staff member is their spouse or when they're actively or aggressively perusing sexual relationships with other residents. We have to figure out if the family is ok with it because the residents are adults with rights, so we have to distinguish between if it's wanted or unwanted. Is someone being coerced? There are many times our clinical teams must address it and document it. There are medications some residents take to lower their libido, but every single place I've worked has had those issues. It's much easier if someone screams or yells NO but that's usually not the case so we must be detectives. We must be very careful with how we approach it. Some residents love the attention will walk hand and hand together into a room. Sometimes we must look away and let things happen naturally because they are adults.

22

"A sweet guy and his wife had early dementia and they moved into assisted living. He would go out to the common area with a blanket or something and would sit next to the ladies and put a blanket over their laps and fondle the hell out of them the whole time. Sometimes he'd put it over two ladies and fondle both the whole time he's sitting on the couch. And you keep an eye on them, *try to distract it, and wonder how much of it is dementia and how much is 'he's just a perv?' Sad thing is the granddaughter worked in management at the community and I had to break it to her 'mama is in the apartment and daddy is laying the fiddle'. But to discourage that, even in memory care, is tricky."*

23

"I worked in a memory care community and a female resident used to go to the bathroom by herself. One day I walked in her room and another resident was trying to shove his penis in her mouth as she sat on the toilet. I ran him off but ever since I keep seeing him try to dominate over her."

They put the moves on other residents, which is to be expected, but it's not ok when they make advances on employees. I have been goosed several times over the years by different dirty-old men. That's what they're called when they grab women, isn't it? Working in assisted living is not for the weak of heart. Some of the stories and secrets they shared were over the top. Some expressed guilt for participating in evil acts and some residents relive memories of being raped however many decades ago. One lady talked about participating in lynchings. Dementia brings out all sorts of memories that are at times vocalized even though the residents likely wanted to take those stories with them to the grave. While working overnight at Whispering Winds Assisted Living one resident in the dementia unit was very advanced in the disease process and she rarely slept. One night she rattled on and on about "lynching niggers." My father is a black man who was born in the deep south in the 1940s, so I didn't have any empathy for her

33

condition at that point. Another caregiver and I sat and engaged with her to prevent her from standing up and falling since that is what tended to happen when she was bored and left alone.

The heinous crimes the 90 something year old woman rambled on about were disturbing and I could tell it wasn't the first time the caregiver heard nasty stories because it didn't faze her. However, it was my first time, and I certainly won't forget her. And, no, she didn't speak about it as if she were being haunted by the experiences. She was more like matter of fact that was her life. Now the past atrocities she committed were out in the open for staff members to discuss in the corners of the community and in the employee break room. And there were lots of stories shared by workers that wanted to gossip anyways. It's probably a good thing that most of the caregivers in that community were young Latinas, Filipinos and Ethiopians who were indifferent to the black-American experience in our country. They only gossiped and giggled about the residents that revealed skeletons in their closets. That particular resident was in the late stages of dementia so she would soon answer to the creator for her crimes, anyways. At least that's what I told myself. Emmit Till's story resurfacing in the news and being showcased in museums forced society to come to terms with the fact that many of the lynching instigators, witnesses and perpetrators are residing in assisted livings today.

When I first began working in an assisted living, I really didn't know the difference between a good one or a bad one. At the time Whispering Winds didn't even have a real name. It was named after the nearby freeway. It took one of the many management companies that came and went over the years for it to gain a real name, that which it is still is called over a decade later. In the four or so years I was there I worked for multiple supervisors, owners and or management companies because of constant change. Not only were companies fading in and out, but the managers came and went even more often. Around every three months, a new executive director started, and it took even less time to burn through nurses, marketers, and caregivers. The only staffing that was consistent in the time I worked there was the maintenance director, the director of dining services, and two tenured caregivers.

The first time I walked into Whispering Winds it was obviously for low-income seniors, yet it didn't wreak too badly of stale urine as so many often do so I figured it was fine. Well, it did smell in the locked memory care unit, but it didn't smell in the assisted living area. The business office manager hired me on the spot; no interview, no background check, because she was so swamped with processing payroll, invoices, resident's monthly payments, and whatever else she had to do to keep the place afloat. There was no executive director or receptionist, and the phone was ringing off the hook which took her away from completing the paperwork that was stressing her out. She desperately needed someone at the front desk manning the phones.

I remember lots of vendors constantly called demanding payment for outstanding invoices. I was told to respond they would receive payment and if they entered the community, I was to call the police since it would be considered trespassing. That should have been a red flag, but I was in my twenties and didn't really know any better. That office manager who hired me contracted her husband to build the beautiful granite-top front desk that I sat behind each day. That was a mistake. I don't think he ever got paid for that desk. A few weeks later she was either fired or she quit but I can still remember her rage as she stormed out of the double glass entrance doors. I was instructed to call the police if she entered the community and although I saw the writing on the wall it was just a job to me back then.

24

---◆---

"A *new management company* took over and had a 6-12 week turn around for paying invoices and I kept getting calls from vendors looking for payment. Even the food company kept calling and my executive director knew because we talked about it every day. He did some investigating and said allegedly there was only one person authorized to sign accounts payable checks and that person was on vacation. I don't know if that was really the case, but vendors were calling looking for their money every single day."

Before I began working there, the parking lot had been repaved at the request of the new owners. The contractor repeatedly called for payment and eventually showed up at the building. I felt hesitant to call the police out of shame. A few weeks after the office manager storming out cursing incident, I gave my two-week notice to one of the owners who often visited. He pulled me into an office and showed me a VHS video (yes, I'm that old) of him giving thousand-dollar tips to cocktail waitresses in Las Vegas. He drove a black Mercedes Benz, and so did his beautiful fiancé who wore pointed high heel shoes and frequented the community with him. I needed the job and agreed to work the graveyard shift, so I didn't have to take vendor's calls. Several months later I became the activity director. The activity position was what I initially filled out an application for, but the office manager pulled me to the front desk. Little did I know not paying vendors on time was standard practice in many assisted livings.

The company that owned Whispering Winds ended up being in the local Las Vegas news for collecting December's rent in a Vegas facility then issuing move-out notices to all the residents a week before Christmas. They all had to be out by month's end. I cannot remember the details, but I saw a clip on the news. I remember watching devastated, evicted residents being interviewed right before Christmas. It was awful, all the while the owners flaunted a wealthy lifestyle and put on a show having the facility housekeeper clean their mansion on the mountain.

Eventually I was offered and accepted the activity director position but received zero training for the new role. All I knew was activities were supposed to happen. So, I lured residents out of their rooms and apartments any way I could. And I quickly learned I needed to announce activities in the dining room emphasizing food and liquor which brought high attendance in activities and planned events. Bring on happy hour.

Alcohol had not been a big part of my life and I really didn't drink until I reached my late 20s. It never occurred to me that some of the residents were alcoholics... and had been for over fifty years. I didn't know about doctor's orders for alcohol or interactions with medications. I didn't know about service plans, and I didn't know which questions to ask. I planned and implemented activities, and every Friday afternoon, a different theme was featured such as Irish Eyes Are Smiling (whisky) and Mexican Independence Day (tequila). Playing the role of an amateur, self-taught bartender with Cocktail pizazz, and zero measuring tools, Mariachi music played in the background while I made Tequila Sunrises and Margaritas and served chips and salsa. The dietary manager made a splash with fancy fruit and cheese tray displays and the residents loved it. One by one, walkers and wheelchairs entered the activity room, and with mild excitement, the senior fun ensued. "A little lower and to the left," shouted one of the elderly ladies who witnessed the groping of a buttocks and made an effort to instigate a tad more excitement amongst the now crowded, silver-haired room. And, one by one, more drinks were poured.

Enter an electric scooter driving at rabbit speed by a man a bit unstable behind the wheel. This resident had recently moved into the facility and wreaked of urine every time he passed me in the hallway. He presented raggedy in his dress with unkept hair and beard. "What'd ya' got to drink?" Jose Cuervo was the spirit of Mexican Independence Day, and I poured the unmeasured ingredients into a red solo cup. After his second drink it was easy for everyone to see he'd had more than enough. The residents knew he was drunk before he entered the activity room, but I was oblivious thinking that's just how he was.

He came back for a third drink, and I politely denied his request because now he was obvious by slurring his words and raising his voice. Then he started shouting while attempting to stand up from his scooter to relieve me of my bartending duties. He fell off his scooter and had no possible way of getting up without assistance. He was still cursing but wasn't bleeding. Unskilled and without a caregiver in sight, I left the scene to find help because I didn't know what to do. As I ran for help, he was still cursing at me for not giving him more liquor.

I found a caregiver who lifted him back onto his scooter, and off he drove down the hall toward the main community entrance cursing all the way. Later that afternoon, communication about his constant drunkenness was disclosed to me by the nurse of the month. "His daughter said he's been an alcoholic all his life. Don't serve him any alcohol." That information would have been helpful earlier that day or when he moved in. A while later he returned to the facility with what seemed to be bottles of alcohol in a brown paper bag. I didn't see the bottles with my own eyes, but I heard the clanking, so I assumed the worst. How did I not notice this before?

25

---◆---

"There were two sons, an attorney going through a divorce, and an accountant. The brothers were co-POAs. The attorney was a raging alcoholic, and their parents were living in a casita for early memory assistance, but they were so far gone they really needed memory care. The wife unplugged the phone every day. The son from out of state would call and say, "there's something wrong with your phone system" what's wrong with your community, every day, three or four times a day. One of the caregivers called and said Shitty Britches is here and I think he's been drinking, and he has brown stuff running down the back of his pants. So that's how he got his name. Sometimes Shitty Britches and his girlfriend would be in the bedroom when the caregivers got there in the morning. There were empty bottles under the bathroom sink of the resident's room.

I did activities for several years at Whispering Winds and learned the ropes quickly. There and for other locations I drove residents to all sorts of destinations such as casinos, museums of every kind, professional ball games and children's ball games, theaters, ballets, symphonies. You name it. We went to see the Nutcracker, the Great Gatsby and Shakespeare plays. On a weekly basis, I took residents out to breakfast and lunch for those who could afford it. At one memory care community I'd get there around 7:15 AM to start up the bus and begin rounding up residents for the outing. By 7:45 AM, the bus was usually loaded, and we'd be on our way to the breakfast restaurant of the week. But one day I will never ever forget, one of the residents hadn't gotten on the bus, yet.

My activity assistant waited on the bus with the residents who were ready to go while I headed towards the missing resident's room to see what the hold-up was. Near his door, two caregivers stood there, and I asked is the resident was ready to go. They replied they didn't know and said they had to hurry to help someone else. I thought nothing of it, knocked on the door then opened it, and thank goodness he had his back turned to me because his pants were pulled down and another resident was giving him a blowjob. I left the apartment a bit traumatized finding the very same two caregivers standing down the hall laughing. They wanted me to walk in on it because they already had.

Working with people who have dementia is very challenging, but they tend to be easily redirected when they're in a good mood. One resident that hadn't spoken for months began singing every single word of Jingle Bells at our resident Christmas party and I remember the joy on her daughter's face for finally hearing her mother's voice again. Another time we brought in zoo animals and placed them on towels in the resident's laps so they could pet them. Another lady who hadn't spoken in quite some time was petting a bunny rabbit ever so gently and something triggered in her mind to say out of the blue, "I have a coat that feels like this." It shocked all of us to hear her speak. One memory I hope to never forget was the time when I was the activity director and I got two residents to bake cookies with me. They both had advanced dementia. In the time it took one lady to shape cookie dough into a ball and put it on the cookie sheet, the other lady would pick up the cookie dough ball and eat it. It was so sweet to watch them. Neither were paying attention to the other, but they were working hard on those cookies that never did make it to the oven.

Living in assisted living doesn't have to be boring unless a person chooses to make it that way because we did all sorts of fun things inside the facility and outside. Sometimes it's easier getting residents with Alzheimer's and other types of dementia to participate in activities and go on outings than it is to get residents without a cognitive impairment to participate. Although we're supposed to ask, sometimes it's better to say, "come on, let's go," rather than getting a flat 'No' answer if we ask if they want to participate.

Activity directors are supposed to do their best to obtain as much information as possible with probing questions to fill out resident's social histories. And, they even attempt to implement what residents and families say they like to do. Yet, there is usually very little participation, except for with BINGO which usually has a healthy-sized group in comparison to other activities. So, what's up with Bingo, anyways? I'd swear every assisted living community I've been in has BINGO on a weekly basis, and some places have it even more often. From the fall of 2006 until the fall of 2010, by resident request, I called BINGO for two solid hours multiple times a week. I was dreaming of calling BINGO in my sleep. Maybe residents like BINGO so much because it's like playing the lottery with low stakes winning candy or dollar store prizes. At least I had greater participation in an activity that didn't involve alcohol.

26

—◆—

"One resident looked great, was well put together, but she would go to the dining room for breakfast and say, well every one of my rings were stolen last night. Lock your doors people. Every ring of mine was stolen. The son and daughter in law would call me saying, "I thought we moved our mom into a safe place." We'd have to go up, and we'd find all her rings. This went on for two years until I finally left. She was still driving but she couldn't find her way home. And family was in denial saying it was just the change of moving from her house. It's been two years, guys! You could see from her appearance; you know that look in their eyes. It was probably one of my hardest residents."

Lonely residents demand tray service to their rooms for three meals of the day and when the caregiver enters residents talk their ear off. Most places charge an additional fee for the luxury of room service with hopes of getting residents out of their rooms to be around people their own age. Residents need positive social interactions, but they have the right to refuse to participate or even watch activities. We weren't designed to be alone 24/7/365 and getting assistance with toileting isn't considered 'social interaction' even though it's one of the most intimate experiences an adult can share with another individual. Most residents simply prefer to remain in their rooms watching television, reading books if they still can, or just staring at four walls doing absolutely nothing while slowly going stir crazy growing more and more depressed.

There's more to life than sitting in the room watching television or only coming out for meals and BINGO. Both residents and caregivers refuse to initiate activities so hiring personnel is the only hope for fun. There's a whole lot more to the activity director's position than simply facilitating games and outings. From planning the monthly activity calendars and trying to implement activities on time, to planning and decorating for events, securing entertainers and volunteers, and ensuring you have all supplies needed, being an activity director can be overwhelming even if you have an assistant. Driving the bus, escorting groups on outings to just about every destination one can possibly think of minus a strip club, trying desperately to get volunteers in to do whatever it is that each volunteer likes to do, and personally getting to know every single resident to grasp what makes them tick, the job description is more extensive than one would presume.

Watching television and waiting for meals or for a caregiver to come into the room to provide care services isn't living a full life. What did that resident do when they lived in their own home? They likely watched television and waited for the mailman or for a neighbor to 'finally' stop by. It's so sad that many elders don't care to have anything to live for. As children we learned and played. As adults we worked and looked out for others. As elders, after everyone is grown and our loved ones have moved or passed away, too many just sit in the house all alone and depressed.

An assisted living professional of 5 years expressed why she loves working in this industry. "To see seniors' live life instead of waiting to die." Some of us try hard to help residents enjoy their days, at least for the small percent of the population that will engage in social activities. Unfortunately, some give up on 'living the best of the rest of their lives' and choose to stay alone in their rooms. Many of them do have ailments which makes them reluctant to leave their comfort zone. Maybe they're blind, or think they'll have to go to the bathroom, so they don't want to travel far thus minimal participation in activities. But some won't even leave their rooms at mealtime.

Recently, I trained an inexperienced activity director who thought the job simply entailed playing games and planning parties. After around two or so hours of uncovering the massive list of expectations by state, corporate, residents and families, that brand new team leader's head was swimming. After around 90 days into the position, he voiced his frustration about the same few people being the only ones that come out of their apartments to participate in activities while most residents reclused in their rooms. He was also utterly disappointed in the caregivers because they weren't interested in encouraging the residents to come to activities. After meal clean-up they would leave the residents in their rooms instead of bringing them back out. Trying to lure residents out of their rooms after they've gotten cozy in them is the hardest part of the job and it often makes activity professionals feel like they've failed. Other tasks associated with the title are planning and decorating for special resident and family events which seem to take place very often in some locations.

Remembering to take pictures during business is a challenge and we must ensure before taking pictures that everyone has signed a photo release, or we must crop-out residents from the background of pictures.

Several residents' pictures could be posted on the in-house community bulletin board but weren't allowed to be posted on social media. Some residents have ex-caregivers stalking and trying to exploit them. Currently I have one family member banned from the community I manage at the request of the durable power of attorney, the daughter. We literally have two photos of the estranged son posted on the wall for employees to recognize him in case he shows up. That's one reason why I like 'secret squirrel codes' numeric locks for doors to help keep the community safe. Only employees should get the code and it should be changed periodically. Estranged family members get banned by legal guardians and powers of attorney all the time, and often for good reasons. One resident had a lawyer on the 'do not confirm the resident lives here' list. Some persistent people will call and visit facility after facility in search of their victim. No last names are allowed on the newsletter so it's, 'Happy Birthday, Lois H.'

27

"For a long time, our sing along songs have been 'Bicycle built for two' and "You are my sunshine'. The songs are starting to change into stuff from the 50s and 60s and that makes me wonder what songs my generation will sing when we get old, maybe Taylor Swift or Beyonce."

28

———◆———

"We have to educate families on the front end. Families should know their loved-one's taste buds are changing and going away. Salespeople should not say we're going to check on your loved one every hour or we never put on a movie. The residents need down time, too. Sometimes people want to sleep-in, and they miss breakfast. We need to be realistic with sales.

During a class I took in Oregon to become a facility manager, a regional director from an anonymous company voiced his opinion which registered with just about everyone in the room of a dozen or so industry professionals. I am paraphrasing, "Many residents expect choice steak and lobster. But when they lived in their own homes, they did not eat steak and lobster all the time." It's true, no one cooks as good as grandma, or even the residents themselves. They prepared and cooked the way they liked it in their private homes. But lobster is not in the budget in most communities unless it's for a special event, and even then, I'd be shocked if it's served.

One of the main complaints in assisted living revolves around the food. Even when there are monthly dietary meetings for residents to attend and voice their concerns directly to the dietary manager or executive director, the main complainers don't attend. Since food is a constant complaint, it also dominates resident council meetings. Food is hardest hit on resident and family surveys for several reasons including powdered mashed potatoes and canned vegetables. Less is better than more with salt. Many residents have high blood pressure and other medical conditions so cooks must be careful with adding sodium a.k.a. flavor. 'Clean' salt and pepper shakers on tables are helpful if they're being sanitized and refilled on a regular basis. Salt & pepper packets may be a better option. No matter what ingredients are used or provided, there will still be complaints and enormous pressure on the dietary personnel who are overworked and underpaid just like everyone else.

Residents complain the service is too slow, the food is cold, and the food lacks quality, variety, options, and presentation. Sometimes dietary managers attempt to incorporate resident and family recipes into their cycle menus. Yet, that's just not good enough. One community I worked at hired an executive chef and still, even his food was the main topic of complaints. Each individual resident has specific taste preferences that no dietary manager or cook can match perfectly for every single resident, every single meal, day after day. Slip up and someone will hear about it. Complaints are constant in just about every department.

29

"It's not good food that we serve. There's just not enough effort that goes into the food. It's obvious the cooks just slap food on the plates. Some servers will serve a resident without wiping the table. There are crumbs and greasy stuff on it. And the entire place is unsanitary. The dietary manager doesn't help, she just tells everyone what to do and we can never find her because she's always hanging out with a caregiver that she's in a relationship with. And she even said the previous dietary manager that hired her told her not to clean certain things, so the kitchen is unsanitary."

Sometimes residents want to enter the dining room an hour before service is scheduled to begin, then they get agitated at not receiving service immediately upon entry. They want their coffee before it's even brewed, and they want to be the first person served since they feel they've waited the longest. Dietary aides are under intense pressure to rush faster knowing some residents get loud and nasty often working up their table mates to complain too. If the server gets into a routine and always begins service at the same table each day, then everyone will hear about it. Residents start arguments and yell in the dining room at each other. They yell at staff members if their food isn't right or if another resident is dressed inappropriately. Mealtime is often the only social interaction residents have with their agemates. It's too bad they won't get involved in fun activities to enjoy life a little more. For Grumpy-Grans at very least it would provide other things to be upset about.

30

"A resident makes my job more difficult on purpose. I'm always calm but she always comes off mad and whining. She has me run back and forth for stupid stuff and her food is never right. There's either too much ice in her drink or not enough ice. She was banned from the dining room and now she's allowed back inside so I want to quit."

31

"One resident makes me contemplate quitting because he comes in yelling, "Where's my dinner?" and God forbid we run out of bananas. I sent one lady's plate back three times and then

she said, "I'm not hungry anymore." There's always someone unhappy and these residents try hard to make us as miserable as they are. It's a normal thing for residents and families to scream at us. The manager said I have to have thick skin and don't take it personally. They yell at us because the wrong thing is listed on the menu, because the food is cold, because the portion size is too small, and for all sorts of reasons. They try to make my job harder."

Being early for breakfast is not always the resident's fault. Limited caregivers hurry to get people up and dressed, escorted to, or parked in the dining room, then they must rush off to help the next person get ready and to the dining room in time. In some communities, the caregivers are also the meal servers since it's simply not in the budget to hire dietary aides. Either way, whether there are dietary aides or caregivers, serving 50-100+ people is just too much for one person to be timely and make everyone happy. Servers must first pour juice and coffee for residents which can take ten to twenty or more minutes. I hate to say it this way but, the time it takes to pour one cup of coffee depends on how long it takes us to cut off a resident in the beginning of their story. Although they know others are waiting, residents behave like 'now is the time to make small talk with busy employees.'

32

"All drinks have to be done in 8 minutes and my supervisor expects you to be done in that certain amount of time. But that's not realistic when there's so many people to serve and some residents take longer to tell us what they want, or they want to talk to us because they come to the dining room to hang out with other

people. My boss, the chef, is really cool but he has to do what corporate says and that's to get the juice cart done fast and to get the food done fast."

With so many people waiting at the same time, it's not a wonder why anytime dining is being tried in some locations. Anytime dining is from around 7AM-7PM allowing for people to sleep in and come back late from appointments without missing meals hopefully eliminating a rush at three specific hours of the day. However, it may drastically alter the staffing plan, and therefore, the budget. Not all companies are ready for, nor willing to implement that shift in dining. Most assisted living dining hours are generally around 8 AM for breakfast, 12 noon for lunch, and 5 PM for dinner, give or take an hour or so. There typically shouldn't be more than 14 hours between dinner and breakfast.

If the cook doesn't arrive to prepare breakfast, then it's up to management to scramble to get the eggs scrambled for all those 'already upset because breakfast is late' residents. By the time management learns they're short a cook, breakfast time is fast approaching. Neither residents, families nor state representatives care about the why. People get rude and even yell caring only for residents to be fed well and on time. But they're upset at the wrong people, the ones trying to pick up the slack due to other's short comings. The only other cook who could cover the shift is likely already scheduled for later that day and/or is already overworked and upset. Salaried dietary managers try to meet the high expectations of residents and corporate while maintaining the meager food budget. There are only so many budgeted work hours in the day, so things get missed here and there even when the kitchen is considered fully staffed.

33

"The dietary manager would leave me and one other person to cook all the food, serve all the residents, do all the dinner dishes, close the whole kitchen by ourselves. We were there from 6am-7pm just running it. I'm still tired. I'm so over it.

Depending on the company, the daily food budget is typically anywhere between $4.00 - $8.00 PRD/per resident day. No matter how many residents are in the community it's easy to know your budget. Let's say there's a $5 PRD with 30 days in a month, multiplied by 100 residents = $500 per day, or just over $15,000 per month in food costs. But that also tends to include paper products, cutlery, and other tools necessary in the kitchen. In some locations, employees eat for free after all the residents have been fed. In other communities, employees must purchase meal tickets at a discounted rate than that of guests, i.e., visiting friends and family members. Most left-over food is thrown in the garbage or dated and placed in the walk-in refrigerator only to be tossed out two to three days later. Sometimes, a creative cook can use the leftovers the following day in soups or other dishes. Many times, food gets forgotten in the refrigerator for weeks which is why health department inspections are important.

I had one cook that literally would use Tinfoil to wrap and freeze leftovers even if it was only the size of your palm. After she left, we found the undated, unlabeled, mysterious tin-foil blobs in the back of the freezer.

34

"*My manager said the residents can only get $2 worth of food for every meal and it's like cafeteria food, very childish food with kid's portions. And we have to take a plate back for more food all the time. I guess the residents in memory care lost so much weight because we were told to load up their plates heavy.*"

35

"*We have to put some resident's food in a blender because they have a hard time eating solid food. It just looks like mush on the plate so now I put each thing in separate bowls, so it doesn't all run together. Sometimes we have to add thickener to their drinks too. My boss said he is going to order food molds for the pureed food, so it looks better because people are losing a lot of weight in the memory care unit.*"

A dietary manager's annual salary is anywhere between 40K-80K depending on the company and potential census of the building. Larger communities allot for larger salaries. Cook's hourly wages averaged $13-$17 before the pandemic. Now we're lucky if we can hire someone who knows how to work a flat top for less than $20 per hour. Dishwashers and servers are totally exploited at minimum wage or just over depending on if they've gotten raises over years. Dishwashing isn't hard but it's very messy, wet, hot, and sticky. It's very overwhelming when you must scrape off discarded food from hundreds of plates and bowls and pour out beverages from hundreds of coffee cups and glasses. Not to mention all the silverware, pots and pans, steam table pans, cutting boards and on and on and on. Just when you think you're done, more dirty dishes appear.

Working in the Pacific Northwest opened my eyes to the growing population of vegetarians and vegans moving into assisted living. On the weekly menus, for decades, I have been so used to seeing chicken, beef, and pork because a lot of residents from the G.I. generation grew up on farms. I was once a strict vegan and avoided eating in common restaurants because of cross contamination so I had an eye to watch and see what vegan looked like in assisted living. The dietary manager tried to create vegan meals for a couple of residents, but the meals were seriously lacking in flavor, texture, and presentation. It was possibly lacking in nutrients too because a lot of the vegan stuff is really processed.

Everything was being prepared on the same cutting boards, in the same pots and pans, and with the same utensils the meaty meals were prepared. The dishes don't get washed properly, simply hosed off and run through a high heat-chemical sanitizer. A soapy sponge never touched the plates, cups, or silverware, ever. Lipstick remained on coffee cups and bacon grease was slimed onto everything. After the pots and pans are washed there was still a greasy film on them probably because dishwashing is messy and hot, so employees want to get through the job quickly. We know stuff doesn't get cleaned properly. We can't blame it on millennials or gen z slacking off because people of all ages working in kitchens do unprofessional things, that's why we have 'This is the way we wash our hands' signs posted everywhere. Those signs are nothing new.

36

---◆---

"Sometimes we take shots after work with the manager, and she gave me a bottle of Fireball whisky even though I'm only 18 years old. She takes videos and it's all on her phone. We have uniforms but I don't wear them. They can't do anything about it because they need me. I've gotten bribes and gift cards; they can't fire me. I've already walked off the job twice and they begged me to come back. They're that desperate. I am guilty of taking advantage by having long fingernails, but I work my ass off, I cook, I clean, I'm dishwashing, I even helped prep for lunch and I'm a server. I have my own duties. And I'm only paid as a server so no matter the job I do my pay sucks. They take advantage of me."

10 budgeted hours per day was at a few communities I managed where the caregivers had to wash the dishes as a daily task. Cook hours were 7am – 1:30pm & 3:30pm – 7pm (this included meal preparation, actual cooking, clean up, ordering, dating, and putting away the order upon delivery). Commonly food is delivered by truck from large food companies based on whatever was previously ordered; frozen, canned, boxed, and fresh food items to assisted living communities on a weekly basis. It is up to the dietary manager to stay within budget when ordering to feed all the residents.

Kitchens tend to have a large freezer, refrigerator, and dry storage for a couple weeks' worth of food supplies. Food is supposed to be rotated first in first out, but some locations don't care or know what's really in their food panties. Inventorying and thoroughly cleaning out the storage spaces tends to be neglected whether due to tenured staff complacency or constant staff turnover. In some locations where budgets rule and negligence persist, professional equipment isn't properly maintained, and pests colonize facility kitchens and resident rooms.

37

"*Me and another guy pulled out jello and pudding packages. It smelled so bad, and there were so many rat droppings and chewings in that box. The manager said throw away what you have to but salvage the other ones. He told us to run the unpunctured bags of pudding through the dishwasher. Me and my co-worker looked at each other and we threw out the whole box because it had so many rat-turds. Then a few months later the menu guy came, and he was there to clean out the dry storage. At first it was fine but about after 15 minutes there was a terrible smell coming out. And after like an hour I was like, Damn! What was in that dry storage? The guy had on two masks, and he came out and said, "can I talk to you outside for a minute?" So, we go outside. He said "You know what I'm cleaning up in there. Probably about 2 years' worth of rat-piss and shit. This isn't even sanitary for me. Who's running this place?" He said he was chipping it away.*"

38

"*When I worked as a cook at Heaven Forbid Senior Living, all together, we caught four rats in the kitchen. One time the server reached up to get the package of coffee off the shelf and a rat*

jumped out at her and she was like, "I quit, I ain't dealing with this anymore!" She stayed a while longer, but she ended up quitting like a month later because everything just kept piling up. When the exterminator came, he was like, "have you seen any lately?" And we were like, yeah, here and there." And then his eyes got big, and he pointed right by my foot and said, "Damn, ya'll got a big one!" And I jumped because he was pointing by me. And I looked and under the prep table was a big ass rat with his head caught in the trap and it was still alive. And I was standing only like two feet away from it because I was cutting fruit at that prep table. At first, I thought he was pointing to a roach, but it was a huge rat. It was like as big and fat as my forearm. I was like, there's no way this is real, but that was the norm at that place until I left."

39

"I was sent to clean the resident's freezers because we're having issues with our walk-in freezer. The walk-in freezer isn't working so we're storing food in the resident's freezers in their rooms. Today we were having peanut butter cookies for dessert, so I had to go to the resident's room to get them out of their freezer."

During the COVID-19 pandemic Styrofoam and other boxed room service trays were being delivered three times a day to dozens, hundreds, thousands of residents, day after day, month after month, for a year or more. We're talking a breakfast tray, a lunch tray, and a dinner tray, for every single resident; a cup, silverware, bowls for dessert or salad. There was so much trash it was unbelievable. Some food would sit out for hours in resident rooms and the next meal tray would be added to the stack of trash.

Instead of taking the old tray away, caregivers would push garbage deeper into the receptacle for it to rot and stink. Food would sit out on countertops and tables, and rot in garbage cans overnight and for many days.

Even when resident's garbage finally got thrown into dumpsters, there was so much trash in the dumpsters overflowing with rotting funk that roaches and rats ruled the premises. It was a mess and bags would sit rotting in the sun. It was a dream come true for roaches and rodents of great length and width. No matter how often city services collected garbage there was still more cuisine to feed the pestilence. Some locations were so bad people complained to the state licensing agencies. But garbage is only collected once or twice a week.

40

"When I first started working at Heaven Forbid Senior Living, I asked my boss what happened to the steel can opener that's supposed to be attached to the end of the prep-table and he said it was covered in roaches, so he threw it out. I was like, why didn't you just clean it. I mean it had a bunch of food on it that's why the roaches were on it, but whatever. And then I started seeing the bugs.

The worst it ever got was when we got the rolling chemical buckets, you know the red ones, we picked them up from under the dishwasher. We picked up the first one and like 15 roaches ran out. The we picked up the second one and like 15 roaches ran out. There was like 40 or 50 roaches that ran out from me moving the barrels and we didn't even pick up the rollers yet. So, we disconnected them, and my co-worker got a long metal pole, and he flipped the wheels over and about 100 roaches ran out because they laid so many eggs and everybody was living in there. And I was like, "we're not doing that again!" And then we grabbed long tongs and grabbed the roller and ran outside in the back and I threw it up in the air. And when it landed it was an atomic bomb of movement. It was the craziest thing I ever seen! There was like 150 roaches and my friend was like, "Move your car! Move your car! because he was scared the roaches would get inside. So, I had to move my car across the street. And then I flung it up in the air again and another 150 roaches came out. And we still had the other two rollers in there.

There was so much water and dirty food and bacteria growing under the dishwasher, it was like free food for em' under there. There were so many roaches. There were little ones and big ones, and like three species that were there. Long skinny like tan-orangish ones, and then there were black and thick ones, and there were hybrid ones. My friend said anytime you find an albino roach it's good luck and we found two of em'. Two albino roaches. I learned roaches molted in the morning. I saw one with antennas still attached to the old skin, their molt is still connected by its own antennas, and I saw the new roach walk away from its old skin.

"I hate doing doubles because it's usually just me and I have to do breakfast lunch and dinner for 100 residents. And people do a half-ass job cleaning up and closing the kitchen at night, so it just makes the roach problem worse. I was like, I need to stop opening up here because I would turn the lights on, and roaches would all start to retreat after a few minutes. I was always fighting the roaches. I'd be chopping something and there would always be one or two trying to take over the cutting board. The last week I worked there I felt something on my neck while I was putting food in the steam table, and I grazed my neck and a roach fell into the hot line food. And it ran out of the food across the little cutting

board in front of the steam table and down under the dishwasher where those red buckets are. I went and told the manager, and all she said was, "Yea, it's bad. You can go home." They probably still served the food because they didn't care."

CHAPTER THREE

Behind The Scenes

While it's evident when walking into a community if it's active with vibrant activities or if it's more television oriented, it's not always evident if the assisted living's internal workings are functioning well with enough properly trained staff. There are many lovely and appealing facilities out there, built with chandeliers, fountains, and all the trimmings. Though visitors may be greeted promptly by a smiling face, behind the scenes are communities in turmoil and residents left without enough caregivers to tend to their needs. There are a lot of good people working in assisted living that try hard to do what's right for the residents and families, often begging for support and funding from corporate invisibles.

Begging brings little reprieve for the managers whose hands are tied. No matter the good intentions to ensure the community is adequately staffed, some assisted livings seem to be cursed. Way back in BC, Before COVID-19, it was challenging to recruit and retain good caregivers. Fast-forward a few years and the entitlement to not-work is unbelievable adding additional pressure to hire and retain good people. Complaints and allegations of neglect and verbal abuse are overwhelming and often justifiable. But sometimes it's the family members doing the abusing and exploiting.

41

—◆—

"An almost 100-year-old lady moved in, vision impaired but she got around and adjusted very well. She ate meals in the dining room with her new friends but didn't participate in activities. She stayed in her room most of the time. Every time her son came to visit, she would be crying when he left. One time she was hysterically sobbing saying stuff like, "I can't do anything right and I'm sorry." It didn't take long to see the pattern, so we convinced her to talk about the situation. Come to find out she was coerced to sign her house over to her son who was living in it and had a gambling problem. Every time he came over it was always for more money.

My nurse was a retired Air Force Veteran, so I had back up when I pulled him into an office and told him he was banned from returning until I complete my investigation. Trespassing I think was the word I used. He started getting heated and my nurse and I were ready to puff up right along with him, so he backed down and left the facility. We reported him to Adult Protective Services. Within days the son moved out his mom and in with him. She was back in her own house, likely neglected, where she passed away shortly after. Adult Protective Services was so backed up that by

the time they investigated the poor lady had died six months prior.
I don't know what became of the son."

42

    "As an executive director memory care is where you have to
be the best listener. One of the worst experiences was when I tried
to convince a son to move his mom from the assisted living into
memory care in the winter in North Dakota. We already had been
letting him know, "mom isn't safe, we found her here, next time it
could be out the back door." Her apartment was situated where
she could have walked right out the back door and there was just
a big pasture out there. I tried to figure out, is it money, what is
the deal? It would be terrible to find your mom on a day like today
60 below wind chill back there and he looked at me and said,
"there's worse ways to die." What do you say to that? She was
such a sweet lady, I said, well you may be ok with that, but I am
not and either we move your mom now or we're going to find
another place for you to take her. What's the relationship there?
Are you mad because you're spending your inheritance? Once we
moved her, he was actually on board and happier because she used
to pretend she knew her way to the dining room and now she's in
a smaller area. She did great. In North Dakota it's just bitter cold
all day long."

43

"As the office manager I was responsible for collecting rent from an adult daughter that had moved her mother into the memory care several months prior. She never responded to any phone calls, text messages, or emails. She didn't pay the monthly rent and we finally had to call Adult Protective Services. After around six months the bill was around$35,000. I think the company ended up having to write it off because they didn't get paid that I know of in the year I was there.

44

"Family wouldn't sign the residency agreement, said "I don't want to be financially responsible," then left and we never got paid. We had two families like that. Moved mom in, moved into her house, never paid any of her bills. Daughter came and picked up mom after we threatened litigation. Took her back to her house with her kids and she died there with no care. And she was the sweetest lady.

Sometimes families don't want anything to do with their loved ones. Then there are over-the-top families that think we can't do anything right or will believe anything a forgetful resident says. It's very difficult to prove if a resident's money was stolen when almost half of the population in assisted living has severe cognitive deficits. What makes it more challenging is most caregivers tend to be new in the community. Even when there are cameras in hallways and common areas, they only hold a certain amount of footage for several days so attempting to retrieve data from several weeks ago may not be possible. We don't normally put cameras in resident rooms for privacy purposes so it's tough to get to answers for families that believe everything their loved-one says even knowing they have dementia. Trying to explain the process to families proves to be challenging for those in denial and for those who think they know everything.

45

"There was a gentleman who constantly would go to a plant and urinate in it. We found out he grew up on a farm and that's what was his normal. We tried to explain to this dementia resident that we were indoors, and he could not pee in the plant. But that didn't work. So, we had to put clothing on him like jumpers that zip up in the back."

46

"There was a lady with dementia in her own universe and she thought she met a friend with another resident that was tired wanting to be left alone, saying "I want to go home." The first lady said, "you're going to sit here with me and play cards with me" and she started screaming at the lady that wanted to leave. Then she grabbed her by her hair and was pulling her by the hair not letting her leave yelling, "she's supposed to be my friend, she's not leaving!" And the caregivers were running up to her yelling and trying to break them apart and it was crazy."

47

"One lady always accuses us of stealing her purse, but she hides it from her own self thinking someone is going to steal it. She always loses her emergency pendant and her daughter calls all the time saying, "My mom's pendant is missing again. I don't understand how you guys keep losing it." That same resident always forgets to use her walker and she falls all the time, and her family blames us like we can sit next to her mom all day and all night to remind her to use her walker."

Years ago, one of the residents was in the hospital and the family came by to pick up some things from the room. They said some of their mom's things were missing from her drawer, so I began an investigation. I figured out a caregiver on the overnight shift was witnessed entering the resident's room even though she knew the resident was in the hospital. There was no need for her to enter the room. So, I held a last-minute meeting on the night shift and had my nurse with me for back-up. the thief was there so I said, "I installed cameras throughout the building so we know who stole the resident's belongings, but I would rather that person come forward rather than me having to call them out."

After the meeting, the employee walked to her car and left, at 10:30 at night. Thankfully the nurse and I were prepared to fire her immediately, so we already had the shift covered. The caregiver abandoned her job, so it was an easy termination process. Now it's standard practice in some facilities to put an additional lock on resident's doors when they're away from the facility for more than a day. Another caregiver sat in the car from midnight until 5 AM arguing with her ex-boyfriend leaving only one other caregiver to help over 90 residents.

It's difficult not being able to trust the little bit of staff you have. But employees aren't the only ones taking things that don't belong to them. She had the brightest blue eyes that pierced amidst her stark white hair. All the snacks, all the napkins, things from desks, whatever caught her blue eyes went into the pockets of her dress or under the seat of her burgundy four-wheel walker. She strolled from room to room collecting stuffed animals, and from common area to common area collecting whatever else. She may have had dementia at that point, but in her prime she was a boss-lady that managed restaurant chains. The sign on the kitchen door that read 'Employees Only' meant 'Come on in' to her. One afternoon the dietary manager was in the kitchen jamming to music while preparing the evening meal. The cell phone with the lovely rhythms playing caught her eyes and ears. She picked it up dropped it down the front of her underwear. Yes, the cook's phone was inside of Blue Eyes' underwear while she walked out of the kitchen door, through the dining room, and down the hall. That technological device was not easy to retrieve… or sanitize.

Right now, I have a resident that loves to collect all the silverware, napkins, and whatever instruments of writing she can find. At least she doesn't go into other resident's rooms like some of the other residents. Someway, somehow all the collectables must be retrieved and returned to their rightful owners but not everything is found. I recall one resident that used to stuff 'things' under her mattress. She also used to take little objects, wrap them in a tissue and flush them down the toilet. Down one of her rings went. Confusion causes all sorts of weird behaviors which is the reasoning behind not bringing valuables into assisted living and memory care communities. The fake stuff looks real enough to secretly swap out. Still, anytime something goes missing we must complete an investigation to rule out wrongdoing.

48

"Families treat us terribly. Honestly working in an affluent demographic those families are super entitled. They pay a lot of money to live there and have their loved ones live there so they're more demanding than any other community I've worked in. Right now, I have one family member that literally is in our community twice a day, and she emails me with lists of everything that went wrong. And asks to know about little things like if nails got cleaned and if hair got styled which is a waste of my time because she already knows since she's there every day. It's frustrating. Especially when the caregivers say the wrong things all the time like, we've been doing it like this forever, and I'm like 'Shut up. You're making things worse.' Employees saying the wrong things triggers issues. Two family members complain about petty things, (has your loved-one's trash been taken out, etc.) and talking about setting traps in odd areas making it difficult for my staff. We stress out when she comes to the community."

Assisted living facility managers are expected to always be 'on' which can make one feel their life is being sucked away because we're always working. Often, we must work long hours with little to no days off because we're on salary (not hourly), and responsible for everything that happens in the community. Staffing, neglect, and other problems are a constant and the last thing we want is to have our licenses taken away or be called into arbitration. Even if someone else is the Manager on Duty, it's still the facility manager who must ensure things run well. But some things are out of our control, so news headlines often feature things like, "2 Dead in Murder-Suicide at Assisted Living Facility", and "Elderly woman choked to death at nursing home by fellow resident." There is only so much we can do. Still, no matter what happens, the facility is still our responsibility. A friend of mine managed an assisted living facility where a male resident committed suicide. Somehow, he secured a gun and shot himself in the head in his room. That incident pushed her over the edge and within months she quit. It was bad enough that she was already burning out from covering shifts and trying to keep families, residents, and employees happy.

Many of us that care about what happens to the residents and our licenses are stuck working as an overnight caregiver after we finish working all day. When there's a last-minute call off, we cannot turn our eyes and allow caregivers to work alone or residents to go without care at night. But I must admit after over 24-hours of being awake and working straight through, it didn't matter to me if there was a last-minute call off right when I finally got home. I could not go back to work without sleeping. My eyes were burning, and I pulled over on the way home to walk around and get a third or fourth wind. That's one of the reasons why a colleague of mine quit after working as an executive director for the first-time. Several months into it, she was a brand-new facility manager burnt out from filling in so many shifts. I felt so bad for her, knowing her pain, knowing how exhausted, frustrated, and abused she felt, as if alone on an island. Knowing her regional director was not capable or willing or going to help her. And I think she had COVID-19 if I remember correctly so she felt miserable.

I voluntarily filled in for her one Christmas eve because she had no to one cover for her. She was way too sick to fill the shift. I, myself, had just covered a caregiving shift due to a last-minute holiday call off. Luckily, she had a caregiver from registry relieve me at around 10:30 PM so I was able to get some sleep. At the turn of the New Year, she left that company and became the sales and marketing director at a different facility. She's still doing sales there today. That's around a $40,000 per year pay cut and it's still a stressful job but she doesn't have to fill in for call-off caregivers.

A different colleague of mine that has interview stories within this very book recently managed a memory care facility and she just became the business office manager at the Christmas eve location. She quit being an executive director, took a $50,000 per year pay cut, and decided to lay low processing Accounts Payable, Accounts Receivable, and payroll. I must admit I think about that kind of thing myself. But the business office doesn't typically pay more than $50,000 or $60,000 a year if it pays that much. And office managers must deal with vendors constantly calling for payment and threatening to cut off services because companies take so long to pay invoices if they pay them at all.

Yesterday as I scrolled a recruiting cite to keep a pulse on our industry, behold Christmas eve is hiring for an executive director, again. The facility opened exactly two years ago. The first and second executive directors left or quit, then my friend last year left, since there have been two more executive directors. Now they're hiring for the role again. In my heart I have a feeling I know whose license will soon hang on the wall at Christmas eve for the following reason: the money as an executive director is much better than that of an office manager and the regional director has probably already thrown big numbers to my friend who just got her first or second paycheck and thought 'this ain't going to cut it.' I am a bit scared for her to take on Christmas eve. Business office, no big deal. Executive director, turn em' and burn em'.

49

"My first time being an executive director, I felt like I needed to fix everything immediately and I was working 80–90-hour weeks totally exhausting myself. My work-life balance was horrible, and I had pressure from corporate office. They would say "thank you for staying so late, you're making such great changes" and I was. But working that many hours I had no time for myself. I did that for 5 months and it wasn't healthy. So, I got to a point where I let go on the staff and management team because they work 8 hours per day, and they leave. But I was staying until 10 PM. So, I had the conversation with my management team like, "Hey, we all need to pitch in a little bit more." They acted like they were on board because they acted like they were glad I was there, but not really. So, I want my community to succeed but I had to set a boundary that I won't work more than 9 or 10 hours unless it's an emergency. And I'm always on call. It's a very hard industry to work in. and it's hard to balance because we're dealing with residents and their families. No job is worth suffering. It's easy to fall into pushing yourself too hard because we're running the whole building and I'm a perfectionist.

50

"I have an interview today. I'm always open to new opportunities which is not my style. My last job I was there 12 years, before that I was in physical therapy for 20 years, I don't like to leave a job, but they run you out. Corporate runs you out, they suck you dry, get everything they can out of you, the *commission is based on NOI (Net Operating Income) and it's unattainable, so I don't even factor in getting a bonus. The SMART goals are a joke. Census teeters, 4 in 4 out every month."* (SMART goals are an acronym for; Specific, Measurable, Attainable, Relevant and Time Based)

The executive director could have the entire community in near perfect condition, a deficiency free community; no citations and all documentation in order. But that only goes so far for if census drops, the facility manager's job is on the line. It doesn't matter how many hours and how hard they work each day, week, and month because business only comes down to the bottom line. Whether there is a marketing director or not, high census is the responsibility of the facility manager. Being an Executive Director may jeopardize one's personal life and health. It can pay well but we work hard for it. Depending on the potential for census and net profit, the company and location, and other factors, executive director salaries loosely range between $50,000 and $125,000 per year. The ones that care about their community earn every penny of it. Yet, no matter how many disaster drills and fire drills we conduct there are some things you just can't plan for.

51

"We had a train derailment with an anhydrous spill. Anhydrous is used in farming for weed killing and it's like a toxic cloud and we lived in a valley. So, I get a phone call in the middle of the night and was like what happened now. And I opened the door to let the dog out and it burned my lungs. So, I turned on the TV and they're like, "put wet towels under your doors, shut off all your heating cooling," and you could see the white cloud rolling

into the valley and I've got all these residents. Thank God my maintenance director lived near the community and was able to get there right away to seal everything off and shut everything down. Staff stay inside, do not go outside! And it's a huge lawsuit. People died trying to get in their cars and get out of there. And what do I do? I get in my car and go to the community. It's like chlorine, it just burns everything. So, I got to the community, and our dietary service director and caregivers lived nearby, and they came in. All these disaster drills we do make no difference if you don't have the people, and a director. Who would have ever thought we'd have an anhydrous spill?"

Managers are burning both ends of the candle trying to make things right for the residents, employees, and families to minimize complaints and move-outs, all the while trying to acquire new move-ins and do everything else. No one should move out due to dissatisfaction. If it's in our power to fix a complaint, then let's get it done! A few months ago, I asked families to give me feedback on my job performance managing the assisted living, opening the floor for them to say what they feel. One family member said, "the executive director should be more hands-on instead of sitting in the office looking busy. And she should wear scrubs and tennis shoes like the caregivers to help on the floor." Apparently, she has no idea how many times I have had to cover for caregivers, and how many reports, emails and follow up phone calls pending that interfere with my 'down time'. And she only visits her dad once a week so to her credit she only sees snippets. Well, I asked for it...lol. How would she know that I keep a pair of scrubs, socks, and shoes in my car because of unreliable caregivers? The Wednesday through Friday MedTech called off for her scheduled overnight shifts. Thankfully a caregiver just texted me saying she can cover two of the three days so I can get some work done during normal business hours. Both ends of the candle, working night and day while trying to prevent complaints.

It's bad enough when one resident runs out of briefs or wipes and another resident's supplies are 'borrowed', hopefully to be replaced before families notice. But it's shameful when resident's personal clothing and linens get destroyed in the washer or are lost due to being washed on different shifts by different members of staff. In some locations 1st shift collected the soiled laundry, 2nd shift washed the laundry, and 3rd shift folded then put away the laundry. Way too many possibilities for loss over a 24-hour period and being handled by multiple personnel with only a magnet on the machines indicating which apartment the clothes inside belonged to. Not only did I get multiple complaints from residents, but families were vexed at having to buy new items. And we won't even discuss why I took away the bleach.

One of the caregivers needed to be on light duty so I made her the designated laundry attendant. She collected, washed, folded, and delivered the laundry on that very same shift. It was wonderful while it lasted as there were zero complaints about laundry. The light duty caregiver knew how every resident liked their clothes washed, and either hung or folded. And, since that was her only job, laundry didn't sit in the dryer for hours getting excessive wrinkles. If only corporate offices had a budget for laundry attendants. But investors don't invest millions of dollars to simply break even. Therefore, busy caregivers or housekeepers need to do the laundry too. Managers will just have to field the complaints, and families will just have to keep purchasing new articles of clothing.

In a thorough community, a specific housekeeping day will be posted in every resident's apartment so everyone, residents, families, and personnel, will be on the same page. It's not enough to simply write a resident's housekeeping day in a service plan that only wellness employees have access to read. If there is consistency regarding days, i.e., apartments 101-120 will be cleaned every Monday, apartments 121-140 will be cleaned on Tuesdays, etc., that would make for efficient communication. But everyone must also be aware it's basic housekeeping services, light dusting, replacing soiled linen with clean and making the bed, cleaning the bathroom, vacuuming, and sweeping and general tidying up. Deep cleaning will not be done, not at least in any community I have ever been in regardless of if I have worked there or not. Some companies offer ancillary service charges for deep cleaning of baseboards and such. Still, I have never actually seen that done. In addition to housekeeping days being posted, mealtimes should also be posted for dignity purposes whether residents are able to read a clock or not. That being the case we rely on caregivers to do meal reminders.

Caregivers are the backbone of assisted living doing everything for the residents. Yet, housekeepers are they eyes and ears of resident's personal space paying a different type of attention to the resident's lives. They provide the personal cleaning services many caregivers don't or won't do. And, neither caregivers or housekeepers tend to want to do one another's job. Not only are housekeepers subject to low wages, just like caregivers, they must clean vomit and disgusting bowel splatters that are not only inside of toilets, but in the bed and on the floor, as well. If the housekeepers are good and trained properly, they will have an eye for, and report, significant changes in the resident's living conditions. And, although we hate to think about scabies and bedbugs, those nasty parasitic creatures live on this planet, too. Bedbugs are often discovered by housekeepers in resident apartments because they change the bedding. Having an eye for tiny blood spots on sheets and elsewhere and checking mattress seams when changing linens should be standard training for housekeepers and caregivers knowing bedbugs are often brought into communities by visitors. Bedbugs arrive when residents move in or return from being out and about. And bedbugs even come by way of our very own employees which is a scary thought.

The concern families had when I sent the message across that we discovered bedbugs in a resident's room was valid. I, and my staff, were concerned, too. But we knew what to do and we took care of the problem right away. It was one room in a well-managed facility but that didn't stop two families from flying off the rails, one of them threatening to move out their mom. Nowadays I'm more scared of families bringing in influenza or COVID-19 than bedbugs. At least bedbugs are lazy hitchhikers that don't like heat. It nearly takes an act of God to convince people to put a mask back on even when they know they have and feel respiratory symptoms.

52

---◆---

"Sweater vest was very odd. His wife had some corporate position and she was on the road a lot. Her mom was a sweet woman who went down very quickly in memory assistance. No matter when the daughter came nothing was ever right, either the sheets weren't right or whatever, it was constant. So, the son-in-law, Sweater Vest, would come every day to check on things and check on us. He's goes into the refrigerator and gets himself food. The caregivers would come into the room, and he'd be lying in bed with his mother-in-law, just resting with her.

We had a knock-down drag-out fight with the daughter. No matter what it was, the food was bad. She was rude and would yell at our caregivers, "Get your ass in here and get my mom cleaned up!" Finally, I had a meeting with her and the caregivers and I said, "they hate when you walk in this building." And she started crying, "I'm just the advocate for my mother." We all understand that but if something isn't right you can talk in a civil manner. And you know where my office is because you're in it all the time. We care for your mom 24/7. The activity on the calendar may not be going on because no one felt up to participate."

53

"If you get too caught up in the compliance and what corporate wants, you're gonna burn yourself out. You're gonna be unhappy and nobody really benefits. Don't try to be a super star. It sounds like not good advice but enjoy your success with coworkers in your community. Don't be such a hurry to tell your corporate office how good you are because it brings a ton of extra work that you're not gonna get paid for. And it takes you away from the residents in your community. Don't try to do more than necessary. Fly under the radar.

The more attention you bring to your community, the more successful, the more they want to knock you down, like, "what makes you so smart." And that's what was frustrating for me because we would work our butts off and share the wonderful processes we put in place, and all files could be impeccable. And corporate would knock us down like, "It's not on the approved form," or whatever.

The pandemic shined a light on who is in it to earn a paycheck and who is in it to be in the service of others. There were no shades of gray in the beginning because employees picked sides out of fear. Staff in the facility were expected to continue providing quality care even when they had the virus while corporate executives hid in corners afraid of catching it as if we all weren't afraid of the unknown mystery illness and what was to come. Corporate could work remotely but someone had to be in the facilities taking care of the residents.

54

"At first, I just felt like this is new for all of us and no one had any answers so just made up my own rules on what we needed to do. When we had our first resident test positive, we closed the doors. We had an apartment right off the lobby with a phone and we put chairs in there, and had the curtains opened, and the families called the number and visited with their loved ones. We booked slots of time, and our team was just on it. But as it got to be from the corporate side it was, "You can't do that, why'd you do this?" Well, there was no direction, so we had to do something. I was one of the first executive directors that got COVID right away. I couldn't be in the building, but I still needed to work so I did it remotely.

We put good practices in place. We're killing ourselves doing things the right way. I took all of that very seriously. I pride myself and my whole career on doing things the right way. You go to the other community, and everything was just fudged. The surveyors just walk in and check, check, check, good to go and it was never done. That was frustrating for me. We're doing it the right way and other places cut corners. Our competitors across the street were falsifying documents and they got deficiency free surveys.

55

"I wasn't supported at all during COVID. They delivered PPE (masks, gowns) but that was it. Way too much paperwork documentation if anyone tested positive for COVID. I had no staff and corporate wasn't willing to come in. They wouldn't come into *the community. My RDO was the only one who came. I basically did resident care the whole time and I couldn't get my normal work done. But corporate still expected me to give them reports on information they can find themselves if they'd open the computer system and log on like I have to do. We're supposed to be keeping residents healthy, and alive, and still trying to provide activities while they're in their rooms in quarantine,"*

56

"*I can't quarantine my memory care residents, they're wandering everywhere. Room trays sit around no matter how often you tell your caregivers to pick them up after meals, so the breakfast tray is still there when the lunch tray arrives.*"

The caregivers know it's in their job description to remove everyday garbage and the last-meal's room trays from resident rooms. They know they're supposed to check and ensure every resident is in the building and provide services to each of them. Information can be available to employees, and even posted everywhere. But will anyone read and implement the information? Here is an example: I have conducted multiple emergency preparedness meetings over the past year. I even have the emergency evacuation information conspicuously posted and inserted in multiple places. We have trained on it numerous times. My employees have signed off repeatedly indicating being part and parcel of the trainings. Yet, just last week I asked two of my caregivers on second shift, "if we must evacuate the building at this very moment, where are we meeting" They looked at me and at each other and around the room. The evacuation information was literally posted up on the wall just behind them.

How much communication and training should we do when people aren't interested in receiving the message? It's easy for important details to slip through the cracks. We even have a 'communication' board so employees can see who, when, and details about people moving in. It's also used to ensure people know when someone has left the building overnight, and to relay other important information. But no one wants to read the board, not the online message board or the one that's posted in the office. One employee was asked how the resident in room number 203 did overnight. The caregivers said the resident was good and she got changed twice. The caregiver was caught in a lie when it was disclosed the resident moved out the day before. Lack of care trumps lack of communication.

Lack of communication is usually one of the greatest problems for just about every assisted living community. Some executive directors are good about communicating and put systems in place ensuring every employee is always on the same page. Many locations hold morning stand up meetings during the weekdays, but there is limited or no management on weekends, thus no stand-up meetings. And rarely have I known of daily informative shift-change meetings during the afternoons or nights. It's unfortunate that way too many locations don't have communication processes in place for caregivers to know when a resident is out of the building or that some residents have triggers that may cause negative behaviors.

Caregivers shouldn't have to be told to notice if a resident is missing five hours after their shift has started. Caregivers should see every single resident on every single shift, multiple times throughout their shift, or find out where the resident is by asking questions. A resident was left to die in a sweltering vehicle overnight, until the next morning and no one noticed. No one cared enough to ask, "who sleeps in that empty bed and why aren't they in it?" Whose fault is that? Is it the person who left the resident in the car? Is it the caregivers' one of whom signed the medication administration record indicating giving his medications the night he was dying in the van? Is it the fault of the executive director for lack of 'Safe Transport" training to employees who likely would be zoned out in a class anyways?

What can we do to ensure employees focus on doing their jobs so no resident is neglected? Here are some of the following items to address to prevent 'breaking-news-worthy' stories being published.

1. How do employees know when a new resident has moved in, and what the new resident likes and doesn't like?

2. How do caregivers working the graveyard shift know of changes in the facility like if a current resident has gone out to the hospital or elsewhere while the caregiver was away from work?

3. How long before the service plan is created so caregivers know how to care for new residents?

4. Do caregivers understand and follow the service plans, and do they document services provided?

5. When there are changes to the service plan how are caregivers informed?

6. How does information about changes of condition get relayed to other departments since only care services read and write daily progress notes?

7. How does a new resident know when mealtimes are, especially for those with cognitive impairments?

8. Is there a proper tracking system to ensure every resident receives a meal, and how much food residents with dementia are eating so weight gain or loss can be better understood?

9. Do non-care providing staff know to watch for concerning changes they may see in the resident's behaviors or living space?

10. If the activity director notices significant changes in a resident, how does that information get relayed to the wellness team to update the service plan?

11. How does the activity director know a new resident is or was an alcoholic and isn't the best participant for happy hour or the wine tasting outing?

12. Do they know about medication interactions, contraindications and physicians signing off on alcoholic consumption by residents?

13. Is the activity director old enough to serve alcohol? And are they trained how to make a proper martini?

14. How do the morning cooks and caregivers know if a resident must fast before a doctor appointment? Whose responsibility is it to ensure the resident is aware and is dressed and ready to go on time?

15. How and when is the cook informed of a new resident's dietary needs, preferences, allergies, or restrictions?

16. How are the resident work orders addressed? Are work orders verbalized to the maintenance director as he/she walks down the hall enroute to fix something only to later forget the several verbal orders?

17. Are mandatory all staff meeting dates and times posted up well in advance?

18. Does everyone attend all staff meetings knowing it's challenging when employees have multiple jobs and obligations? How does everyone stay on the same sheet of music?

19. Is there a check system to validate every resident's whereabouts every few hours, and much more often for residents with dementia?

57

"*My favorite position was an Area Executive Director because I would be in one community for a week to fix a few things then be sent somewhere else the next week. I don't want to hang my license anymore because these places are a mess. They hire people who don't know what they're doing, or they don't give a crap and it goes to hell. There is way too much to clean up and I don't want to put my license in jeopardy.*

58

"*The executive director was never there. He was at the casino every day and the caregivers were a nightmare. They had their kids there, running around, eating all the food, eating off the residents' plates and boyfriends coming in at all hours of the night. They were leaving residents by themselves to go out and party. I was hired to clean it up and be the executive director of 190 residents. The entire community was all one level, hallway, hallway, hallway, skinniest I've ever been working there. It started small and they kept adding on and adding on. And the room numbering was a mess. One side of the property was double occupancy rooms for*

Medicaid and that was the older part of the building. And then the memory care was in the back of the parking lot, like a cottage, basically. They just kept adding wings. Both my mom and my mother-in-law lived there at one time, but not when I managed the place.

The dietary manager was rough around the edges, very crude, an HR nightmare. I told her I really should be firing you for this. She talked to one of the young servers in the kitchen and said, "How can you have bigger boobs than I do? That's not fair. You little girls come in here and look those big boobs." She prided herself on, "they all just love me" but was so unprofessional. Hard worker, but no life skills. Years later she said, thank God, you gave me a chance because I've learned. She would've been sued.

59

"The executive director in a memory care community was having an affair with a number of his staff members in the community. The female staff members did not know he was having multiple affairs so when they found out, that was when all hell broke loose. The women involved became upset, and one went to corporate to turn him in. This was not the only place it had happened. When he was fired, he went to another community and one of the female staff members followed him to the new location thinking she was going to be his one and only. However, that didn't work out. His behavior continued in his new place of employment, and he got fired from there too."

60

———◆———

"After I started the technician said to me, "Why is it that since I started there aren't any problems with the cameras? With the last guy we were here every week because the cameras were broken". I didn't know the marketing director was screwing my predecessor. So, I walked into that. And no body's telling me. Finally, I got some managers to tell me, and they were like, "Oh, you didn't know?""

CHAPTER FOUR

S.O.S. Sales Only Sales

M y first encounter with Ghost Town Senior Living was as a business office manager of a memory care facility. I was being cross trained by the marketing director to step in during a leave of absence. Out and about I was introduced to marketers from other companies who spoke of an assisted living nearby that was a ghost town. What they were saying, more like joking about, sounded pitiful for the residents, and they were adamant about showing me how deserted the place was. So, several of us drove to the community, rang the doorbell, and waited in the foyer for what seemed to be around ten or so minutes. Point taken, no one was around but the lights were on. Eventually, we saw life. A caregiver opened the door, didn't say a word, not even as much as 'hello', and quickly walked away. We then stood in the living room for another five minutes. No managers, no caregivers, no residents in sight, and now we're locked in a secured facility. It took another 10 minutes to be set free.

Fast forward time and wouldn't you know my first interview for an executive director position ended up being at that very same ghost town. The regional director who was interviewing me was the only person around. No residents or employees were in sight. He had received a promotion so was seeking to hire his replacement but for a community two hours away. I accepted…for an entire month. That's how long it took for me to be summonsed to manage the ghost town by my house. It was a good thing I hadn't moved yet.

As the new executive director, I was eager to breathe life into the community and that is exactly what happened. I was on a mission to be successful since I was new to the position, and I worked long hours because I didn't receive much training which meant I needed to find my way through the weeds. So, I was basically in a position to sink, or paddle really fast to churn that milk into butter – Catch me if you can. 'Figure-it-out' was standard for new directors, or at least in that company until I became the designated trainer. I spent extra hours learning how to navigate the company's systems and becoming versed in regulations and leadership books.

The overhead was more than twice as much as the revenue, so the sister properties were holding up the building. The activity director had activities going on but way in the back of the community where no visitors could see the fun that was happening. They were using a high price staffing agency to fill in the schedule holes since there were barely any caregivers. Later I learned a resident died in one of the outdoor courtyards because no one knew he was out there. After the incident the company rebranded. Yes, this was the new company I had just signed on to - with a different name and logo after being one of the companies called out in the PBS documentary.

After only five months, the low census in the community rose significantly. There is no way I can take the credit for what my awesome marketing director did. I simply changed the culture of the community, so it was no longer laughed at amongst colleagues and called the ghost town. Changing the culture made it much easier to not only sell, but to retain residents and team members. It was my nurse and care team that kept everyone healthy and happy as I was in the operations seat and didn't provide much hands on care. Now when the marketer brought in tours, people were around laughing and enjoying life. The census grew. My strategy: bring activities to the front living room so when people visit, it will be evident there are fun things happening instead of simply handing an activities calendar to a prospective family touring. Activities are just as important as care services and food quality. We came up with strategies that contributed to making life easier for sales, and we began building a great team alleviating some of the staffing problems. The position still made me want to pull my hair out though.

More times than not, I questioned my sanity for remaining in the executive director position, especially when it came to hiring, creating the schedule in accordance with the budget, and dealing with caregivers that would quit for a few pennies more an hour to work for the many competitors up the road. At least I had one good thing going: the original activity person left because she didn't like change, and I hired an-inexperienced activity director who never said, 'I always do it this way'. We created a fantastic activity program and vibrant activities were happening front and center throughout the day, fresh baked cookies, and all. We also did things to improve employee moral ensuring the caregivers, cooks and other frontline staff knew they were appreciated. We still had serious staffing problems and had to always hire and train new caregivers all the time. It was a revolving door from day one. If a caregiver needed a day off, there was usually no one to cover the shift. So, day off denied, vacation was denied due to lack of coverage. They tended to just call off anyways so I would be left holding the bag.

The budget allowed 2-3 caregivers to 23 residents, many that had dementia. It was an unsafe staffing ratio which made the caregivers indifferent, and the residents could sense it. The ratio was for profit margins figured into a care level point system software which equated five minutes of a caregiver's time per point. Many corporate offices use software systems to determine how long helping a resident on the toilet should take, as if it can predict stomach aches. As if software can determine how often 'frequent-pee-bodies' will need to be taken back to the bathroom. And as if taking care of people with serious medical conditions and dementia can be put into framed minutes. Leaving an unbalanced and confused elderly resident with macular degeneration on the toilet while rushing to help another resident due to time constraints is a fall and litigation waiting to happen.

How long does it take a caregiver to assist one reluctant resident with Alzheimer's dementia to agree to take a shower, then encourage the resident to get undressed, drain their catheter bag, then actually get them into the shower, then physically wash all their parts, then dry off the resident, dress the resident, comb their hair, brush their teeth, put in their dentures, put on their compression stockings or socks and shoes, making sure their hearing aid batteries still work, and their glasses are clean, and finally get the resident to the dining room for breakfast? Multiply that by dozens of residents between the hours of 6AM and 8AM. Two hours. How many caregivers should it take to get 23 incontinent people up and dressed for the day, and into the dining room so they're not late for their first meal of the day?

The computer software sets the caregiver resident ratio and budget, yet executive directors are held personally responsible for serious situations that occur in the facility because it's their license that hangs on the wall. If corporate isn't willing to pay caregivers and pay for the community to be staffed according to the realities of borderline nursing home services being provided, and something terrible happens, it's the manager's fault. Corporate deflects and will fire a manager to cover their butts. Rarely will a company pay for a manager's legal fees and go to bat for that manager to be able to keep their license.

It's unfortunate my corporate office had unrealistic expectations because it ran off our regional director, the same guy that hired me. He knew it was unsafe. And I recall being told that only one caregiver could be on shift overnight. One person to assist more than a dozen people, unless there was a two-person transfer then there could be two people working. So, let's put that into perspective as we did with the shower points/minutes. If a resident rings their emergency pendant in the middle of the night needing assistance to the bathroom and the caregiver responds. And then a different resident rings their pendant because they've fallen on the way to the bathroom (yes, this was an actual situation that occurred while only one person was working) how is it safe to leave the first resident on the toilet while calling 911 and trying to handle that whole fall situation alone? Additionally, that one person cannot take a break, not for lunch or even for 15 minutes. They cannot leave the facility during their entire shift because the residents cannot be left alone. It was unsafe for the residents and the caregiver. But we did it, we lifted the curse off the ghost town. We got the census up to 50% for the first time since rebranding after the documentary.

Eventually I accepted a promotion to traveling operations specialist, training new executive directors and being an interim fix for facilities without. That was a great position for me since I loved traveling and fixing things. Even my husband knew I loved it because when my alarm clock went off in the morning, I didn't hit snooze for the first time, ever. Three years later the new executive director made a mess of the revived ghost town and there were complaint investigations that prompted the state licensing agency in resulting in citations. I was called to be the interim executive director to do more CPR on the assisted living.

The first day I arrived back at Ghost Town Senior Living we had a 'corporate' meeting in the back room with now another new regional director, our boss, the regional and divisional nurses. They were about to fire the new executive director who turned out to be, well let's just say having negative behaviors. Not only did she not apply any of the training she'd received only a few months prior, but she and the new nurse seemed to be sabotaging the community. Those two behaved like best friends but they didn't like anyone else. The only long-term medication assistant, who had been there for five years, for the first time was a no call no show. I remembered her well enough to know it was not in her personality to simply not show up. She had never called off when I worked there. She was a wonderful team player who had a positive attitude, and I still had her phone number in my cell phone. The nurse and executive director accused her of stealing narcotics. They didn't like her nor some of the other employees, so people were quitting left and right. I called her and she agreed to return since I was there, and the crazy person was gone.

By this time, there were hardly any caregivers left. So, we needed to contract with an outside agency to send caregivers to cover shifts at the expensive rate of $20 per hour. This was back in 2017. (Side note, post pandemic the hourly rate is over $30 per hour). It only took two days before the crazy nurse was a no show and that was great. But it left the community without a nurse or a stable executive director other than me sitting in as an interim. I didn't want the executive director job at that community again.

Regional nurses filled in as they could very sporadically since they had to be in other troubled communities. We eventually had to rely on an even more expensive nurse registry company to send an LPN just to pass medications in the evenings, at night and on the weekends being the registry caregivers couldn't do it according to the state regulations. We needed to hire an executive director, a nurse, a cook, and a whole lot of caregivers and medication assistants. The marketer was new, having started a week prior, and was also new to the area. It was probably better that there weren't any new move ins on the horizon. But corporate didn't like that at all.

Not having a nurse to oversee care services, or enough caregivers to provide the actual hands-on care to residents resulted in having to contract third party agencies at top dollar to fill in the gaps. The agency employees popping in and out didn't have time to be oriented to the residents, the layout of the community, or life safety procedures. Half the time, they didn't put much effort into providing care services to the residents who were strangers, but we need warm bodies to cover last minute call offs. Since there were always new 'fill in' caregivers we could only hope their hearts weren't cold. That's who we had to care for the residents.

Other than staffing issues, which are a constant, my first order of business was to get service plans for the residents, and credentials and training for the employees we still had. We were without a license on the wall, and we couldn't use my license since it was still hanging in my prior community that had the most awesome nurse and marketer maintain quality care and 100% census. We were the best Trifecta in the western division in our time. Anyways, one day at a time, meds were being passed, sometimes late, but at least it was being done. Resident charts and personnel files slowly began coming together. But it took time since I am only one person and was without a solid team. No nurse, no executive director, and a brand-new marketer from out of town.

My regional nurse was able to pop in occasionally, but she was spread thin with several other buildings to cover. We were still looking for an executive director and the brand-new marketer was already being put on a PIP (Performance Improvement Plan) since she didn't have any move ins. She didn't know the area but was pounding the pavement and putting forth effort to learn and produce.

While up to my elbows in correcting the many deficiencies, the regional director called me saying I needed to fire the marketer since she wasn't producing. I stated, she just moved down here, doesn't know the area and is a single mother of a small child. But that didn't matter. So, with a heavy heart, I had to retrieve her keys, phone, and laptop, sending her on her way. Thank God, a few weeks later she got an even better job doing marketing for a Hospice company making much better money.

A day later, I got another call from the regional director telling me to remove my license from the other community and hang it at Ghost Town. I knew of its potential, so I buckled in for the rough ride...until I was told to drop operations and to devote all my time to sales and marketing. Drop ops and produce move ins. Hanging my license there was not a problem if I could continue to get the community on the right track. But there was no way that I felt comfortable about spending all of my time devoted strictly to sales knowing I didn't have a nurse, I didn't have enough caregivers, it was possible I would have to work the night shift, and state survey just left the building the day before I arrived. There were all sorts of bad marks on the report card that I needed to write 'Correction Plans' for. I replied I would spend half of my time in operations, and the other half doing sales. At least I knew the area and referral partners. That wasn't good enough so both the regional and our divisional called me on three-way demanding I drop operations entirely and focus solely on sales. By then, my license was hanging on the wall, and I was desperately seeking coverage for overnight shifts. If one of the caregiver staffing agencies didn't hurry up and find coverage it was going to be me working them. It was already late in the day, and I was not happy. I remained calm and professional on the phone and replied, "I am not interested in getting into trouble potentially having my license taken away so I will continue to fix the compliance problems half of the time and do sales the other half. 50/50 sales and operations"

I felt pressured so I got human resources involved a day later. Then another phone call from my boss who was on the line with the regional director and the human resources person I had voiced my concern to. All three demanded I drop operations and focus solely on sales or be written up. We all politely and professionally ended the call. The issue was harder pressed for me to drop ops and sell, sell, sell, and it was three against one. I was responsible for the community, and I no longer felt secure with the company. We didn't have enough caregivers to care for the residents already in the building and they only cared about me bringing in more people. Corporate didn't care there wasn't anyone to work the shifts and they never entertained the thought of providing hands-on care in the facility themselves.

Scheduling is the executive director and nurse's problem not the corporate executives. But there wasn't a nurse, or an executive director. There was my license on the line, so it became my problem. I was heartbroken because I loved my job, but they pushed too hard and cared nothing about care. The only thing that mattered was high census. Although it was a decade ago that I managed what was once a ghost town, the facility goes through ups and downs and finally got to 100% census for the first-time a few years ago. I couldn't help but feel happy for the team that got it there. Several months later the executive director was fired under mysterious circumstances and the marketer left shortly after.

61

"They will kick your carcass into the parking lot and there will be someone else in your chair. But we've fooled ourselves to think we're indispensable. There were times for me in all my positions, when you get through a survey and you do so wonderful and you think to yourself, "Wow, we did pretty good." And they don't care about that. I cared more about that. I look at it like "look how well we're caring for these residents." Just the preparation we did, my poor management staff were like 'how can we comply with all of this?' It's overwhelming. And that was state. Then you go into joint commission and that's crazy stuff. It's so defeating. Then you write a plan of correction, and no one ever mentions it again."

62

"When I first got to the building it was in such disarray because the previous director either never had control, somehow lost control, or never cared to have any. Caregivers made their own schedules, she let them rule and completely run their own department. There were no citations in the building, deficiency free survey. It was so bad that two months in I told my regional director of operations (RDO) that I won't hang my license on the wall if I don't get a new director of nursing (DON) because I can't fix this on my own."

Occupancy averages around 90% at the assisted living I currently manage which means I have 'rooms' available. Many residents are on Hospice, one actively transitioning, and since this is a business, I must line up someone to take that room right after she passes away. As the executive director I develop relationships with residents and families having compassion in their final moments, and I charge a daily rate for the room until their personal belongings are removed. What a weird feeling, to keep flipping the switch! "We love hugs here. There's a late fee attached to your rent." I am responsible for growing and maintaining census even when I have a sales and marketing team. And there is a lot of competition, so it hurts to turn away incoming leads.

We have no issues accepting people with all stages of dementia. Un-equipped, untrained, and unauthorized to perform medical procedures, I'm not supposed to move in people who need continuous nursing services. Yet denying move ins due to high acuity makes it a challenge to keep the building full since people move in towards the end of their lives. If I admit a resident more appropriate for a nursing home who may further decline and we are not trained or licensed, or staffed to accommodate their needs, I put all the resident's lives and caregivers backs in jeopardy. And my license, and the facility license.

The staffing part is usually the biggest problem, relying on disengaged workers to care for people at the end of their lives. Too many caregivers are unskilled, unreliable, unwilling, and sometimes all three. But I still need new residents to keep business going. I'm selling the hope that we will always have skilled caregivers that will show up and care for residents.

Since the COVID-19 pandemic just about every incoming inquiry is for people that may be more appropriate for a nursing home. They're bed bound, cannot bear any weight to pivot so they're a two-person transfer, they have catheters, ostomy bags, feeding tubes, pressure ulcers, aggressive abusive behaviors towards staff, and serious illnesses and medical conditions. And they have dementia or a disease that may soon cause it. I literally just got texted for a new lead that reads, "SNF (Skilled Nursing Facility) discharge tomorrow, completely bed bound, not eating freely, feeding assistance, difficulty swallowing, full assist with bathing, grooming and incontinence care. "Assisted living started around four decades ago to provide 24-hour assistance with non-medical services, including medication management, known as 'activities of daily living' (ADLs). Only a decade or so ago families who inquired about assisted living sought help with medication management and incontinence care, even stand-by or hands-on assistance with showers. Now we're training our caregivers to work with medical devices.

With so many people having dementia and mental health problems, it's in every one's best interest that assisted living facilities remain secured with locks on all exits because 'has cognitive impairments' makes up around half of the inquiries, and a third or more of the residents already living there. 200% increase, that's how much we anticipate dementia to increase in our lifetimes. Many people are much more than just forgetful or confused, dementia diagnosis or not. That wasn't the case in 2005. Dementia was around but it was not predominant in facilities so there were small wings dedicated to it. Maybe a specialized 'memory care' facility here and there. Today, dementia facilities are springing up everywhere. And so are behavioral health facilities. Some locations have a memory care facility, and across the parking lot is a geriatric-psyche inpatient unit.

At the moment I don't have a marketing director, so everything falls on me. I'm selling an expensive product with a secure environment and quality care. And I literally just got a text message from my nurse that we had a no call no show. The caregiver ghosted us! How can we possibly take care of high acuity residents, many of whom have dementia when people don't show up to work? Just when I think I can enjoy a Sunday off. The current residents cannot go without care. Someone, preferably multiple caregivers, must always be in the facility, and awake. And they should be doing what's in the best interest of the residents when they are there, like working. And this is what we're selling.

Tomorrow is Monday, Independence Day. I guess it's a long holiday weekend that is more important for caregivers to enjoy away from work, but not as important for the residents wheelchaired to the dining room for the $150 guitar entertainment singing battle hymns and the national anthem. The little hand-held flags are already sticking out of the centerpieces in anticipation of the mocktails and treats.

63

"Keeping corporate happy, keeping families happy, keeping caregivers happy, everyone has their ridiculous expectations, the executive director is squished in the middle, and I think that's why they keep turning over. You can't be everything. That's what made me want to quit. Everything is dumped on the marketer and executive director. "You are the champions of marketing so you should know every detail about your leads." And the sales software doesn't talk to the care planning software which don't talk to the billing software so the programs don't talk to each other and you're bouncing around just to find details for their reports."

Inquiries usually go something like this; The caller says, "my loved one or my client falls and forgets to take medicine. The caller provides a few more details about needed services and wants to know how much it costs to live there. The inquiry now comes in daily to thousands of assisted livings across the nation commonly by way of social workers or referral agencies. Each location's representatives have intentions to do what's in the best interest of the inquirer. However, after moving in, things do not always go according to 'best intentions' for all sorts of reasons. Most of the time the marketers and executive directors have tremendous confidence in how great it is to live there, and they really want things to run smoothly.

When tours come into the building staff have been instructed to smile and say hello. Some have even been taught to give their 30-second elevator commercial. During the initial call and tour, families either spill their guts about the extent that their loved one needs care, or they withhold information regarding the real physical, medical, and cognitive state their loved one is in because they just need placement to happen, Now! ... last-minute crisis inquiries. Many times, families don't have the time or energy to deal with this or are in denial about the care that's needed. Families want the right place and management wants high census.

Reassurance that the assisted living can not only meet but exceed resident's needs may be more than the marketer or executive director can ensure. There are often unrealistic expectations from residents and families due to paying thousands of dollars a month. There are not enough reliable workers and there are last-minute call-offs and no shows, so care needs go unmet after moving in, leading to complaints. The faulter in staffing leads to scheduling challenges and caregiver and nurse burnout resulting in frequent turnover. There are always complaints, even in the best communities.

Years ago, I was the marketing director for an assisted living facility that had around 100 residents, most of whom were on Medicaid. Two weeks in I had to give notice after learning there was 1 caregiver and 1 med-tech working overnight. Neither of them knew anything about a resident who had fallen, couldn't reach his emergency pendant, so he banged on the wall…all night long. Reports of 'someone banging' rang from other resident's pendants due to them being disturbed by the noise. But still, no one thought to investigate where the banging was coming from because they were 'busy' for the entire 8 hours, hopefully changing the incontinent residents. By the time I got to work around 8 AM the resident was being wheeled out on a stretcher to be taken to the hospital. That's when I knew there was no way I could feel comfortable about 'selling' that facility. The executive director was burnt out from pulling long shifts and dealing with corporate and staff drama, so she quit only a week after I was hired. I don't blame her for quitting because that place was a mess and that's why I resigned just after her.

Some locations may look good and have well-versed marketers but are in worse shape than you'd believe with resident drug addicts inviting homeless people into their rooms, consuming, and selling drugs in their apartments. One acquisition didn't look bad from the outside or even on the inside. But with all the staffing and management changes before the takeover, it was a free-fall of no accountability. I mean, how can there be squatters residing in empty assisted living rooms? I remember the interim executive director had to kick out the squatters from upstairs units. Residents had the side doors propped open and no one really knew who lived in the facility versus who was homeless. It didn't seem that the caregivers even cared if homeless people lived there.

In that same community, around a week into trying to straighten it out we learned of the neglectful death in the memory care only a month or so before my company took it over. They knew nothing of it, or of the issues in the many other buildings they acquired on the same day. Apparently, one of the dementia residents went outside in the middle of summer when it was over

110 degrees. None of the caregivers noticed and she died outside. Even if she had an emergency pendant to call for help to get back inside, she had dementia and probably couldn't remember to press it. When she was found, her temperature was so high it didn't even register.

64

"On average it takes 12-15 minutes for call buttons to be responded to, when I got there, it was 35 minutes. And we have a small building, but caregivers don't have their pagers on them, they're always lingering around, 4 on lunch and 1 on the floor, concierge is 8a-8p, MedTech is supposed to carry portable phone but won't carry it, pharmacy is at the door, but phone isn't in their pocket."

Sales and Marketing is not responsible for the back door, moveouts and deaths. But that front door better bring in tours that convert into move-ins to keep business going. Like it or not, most residents in senior living facilities eventually move out or die so marketing must hit monthly quotas focusing on net growth. For newly hired marketers, there is an unspoken 90-day rule; within the first 90 days of employment, they'd better increase the census, or they'll be put on a performance improvement plan (PIP) or be terminated. For facility managers, it may be longer, but the same expectations apply even if several residents die over the course of a couple of months and there aren't enough new move ins to net census growth.

Over the years I have seen several marketers get fired within their first three months of working in a community; if census doesn't grow, it's time to go. Firing the marketer is one of the hard conversations for administrators to have: 'Well, yes, I know you've been awesome but corporate doesn't like you from the spreadsheet so turn in your keys and laptop. I'll walk you to the door and we'll mail your final paycheck within the state required number of business days." Business is business, heads in beds.

For an entire year, there could be net growth every single month. The marketer and executive director could be the rock stars of the company having maintained 100% census all year long. Yet, if census drops and there is any stagnation for an extended amount of time, meaning two or three months of low census, their jobs are on the line. The only way to pay the bills and satisfy investors is to always maintain high occupancy with a waiting list so when residents die there won't ever be days of lost revenue.

65

"The cloth furniture looks disgusting and has stains. We lose sales because other places have nicer furniture. It's dirty, it's not sanitary, it looks nothing like our website, I showed pictures to the corporate bosses, and they even agree but new furniture still hasn't happened. And our sister property got brand new furniture last month because their census is full."

66

"*Rooms aren't rent ready. Some rooms could be rented but they look terrible. They sit empty for months and even years with messed up door frames and tattered carpeting that looks disgusting. I can't show that apartment. Sometimes I'm told the apartment is rent ready and it hasn't even been touched up or cleaned.*"

67

"*In this field it does not matter how much you give they still want more. I filled the place up, I did what I was supposed to do, and I about had a nervous breakdown, and my health went down the toilet. and I wanted to quit the industry then, but I didn't. I got a new job, worked at another community, worked at a few other communities after that. Worked a couple of years at each then moved on.*"

I recall a social media post of an assisted living industry professional who spoke of marketers and facility managers walking out or being fired because of diminishing occupancy. Most of the readers who commented agreed the problem starts from the top for too many head honchos think they know what's happening from a thousand miles in the sky.

The turnover rate for Marketers is a few years, and in some locations less than that. To meet what is at times unrealistic expectations by both 'corporate' and families, marketers barely hold on to their jobs while trying to please both. Their average salary ranges between $40,000 and $80,000 per year, plus they receive bonuses or commissions on each move in. Yet, some work more than 50+ hours per week due to being the first to answer inquiry calls within a half hour of the inquiry. Yes, the pressure is on. Exceeding monthly quotas for move-ins and census for the demographic area and being greater than the rest may still not be good enough to maintain a marketing job. No matter how hard they work and how successful they are at filling up the building, 100% census may not be good enough if there isn't a waiting list to go along with it. "Who is lined up to take financial possession the day the furniture from the last resident is removed?" The successes of the past have nothing to do with a current census. It's not all about the marketer's achievements, but what the marketer must continue to achieve. And even if they continue to achieve 100% census, that doesn't entitle them to a raise in pay.

68

"If you're not consistently making your numbers right after you start working then you're out of a job. Marketers come in with little to no experience, not trained on the database, not knowing how to do their job. Most regionals don't even see their marketers except at the conferences which are sales hoorahs. Corporate marketing people don't support, they want a report. Always upping the ante, what can you do to differentiate yourself from the competition? How do we differentiate? What is your staff doing so that tours are really good? How do we present a community well when we've got a naked man running down the hallway, screaming and yelling? Staff is overwhelmed, and staffing is an issue, and we're expecting them to smile pretty for the tour?"

Corporate executives really don't understand because the marketer is trying to do everything they're told to do, and the executive director is trying to keep it all afloat from census to coverage to care to food to activities and budget oversight and then they say you need to make everything look perfect for tours. And when they don't get the numbers, they fire them. That's common. Many people that get hired have no experience in assisted living or elder care. Managers hire new people off the street because they say they really like working with seniors. Some don't have the first clue about the field that they're in, dementia, the aging process or even senior living for that matter so they must learn quickly. Those that have been in the jobs for years are usually really dedicated to what they're doing. But it's disheartening because we're promising care we can't deliver knowing resident acuity is so high and caregivers are in short supply.

For all the time-consuming outreach visits to discharge planners and social workers, and meetings, messages, and phone calls with often confused or distressed families, assisted living marketers are mentally exhausted and stressed out just trying to advance the inquiry into a move in and keep their jobs. They create the faith and confidence needed to believe in the product they're selling even answering lead inquiries at night and on weekends. After all the time and heart poured into the job spending hours documenting every touch; call, visit, email, tour, etc. in each respective company's tracking database, and have a certain pipeline lead to tour to move-in ratio...Literally begging for business from other providers, the best marketers get fired or quit because of spreadsheet failure. At least assisted living tends to be needs based and not simply a lifestyle change. There are a lot of people being discharged from skilled nursing facilities or who should no longer live at home alone in solitude that need the socialization and around the clock care offered in assisted living. Needs based; it should be easy to sell.

69

"What's the census? Give me your stats. What are your projected move-ins? What's your lead to tour ratio and tour to move in ratio? How many calls did you make? How many rings, how long did it take, how many touches, how much outreach have you done, what kind of events are you planning? Marketers don't have support, they have reports. That's the way we explain to our investors what's going on. Marketers are expected to do outreach, lead tours, make sure phone calls are being returned, and follow up on leads. They also attend and create events for the community itself. Sometimes there's a move in coordinator inside of the building. When I started, we worked between 9-12 hours per day, we also work on weekends. Marketers have quotas to meet and budgets or spenddowns to maintain.

We have young adults coming into the business. Quite a few of them don't have an understanding of aging and the aging process. So, they have a lot to learn but then they are immediately saddled with census. Census is king in every single community. If a community is full then nothing else matters, that is the goal. If a community is 80-85% or under that's when corporate and investors start to sweat. Marketers are always striving to get to 100%, that is the goal."

4

In the last 100 years science has empowered longevity to increase. People are living longer but their quality-of-life sucks having to swallow a bunch of pills before breakfast or be pushed around in a wheelchair. While a small handful of 80–100-year-olds still have their wits and are mobile with a walker, the majority are cognitively falling apart and physically dependent on others for everyday care needs. People are less physically active than before, many suffering from obesity and co-morbidities. And they tend to take multiple medications increasing their fall risk and the need for the personal care services that are offered in assisted living. Some facilities are built right next door to competitor facilities, shiny new pennies with covered driveways.

70

"I think we misrepresent it to smart seniors that this is your new home. It's just assuming because it makes us feel better. I managed a beautiful, assisted living. Everyone wanted to live in the fancy place. There were three stories of glass and it looked out over the whole valley. The furniture was top notch. That was the most fun I ever had, building, and furnishing an assisted living. We had a pub in the lower level with a beautiful big bar and we attracted a lot of the very affluent and active people. They were known in that community, the silver foxes. The dining room was gorgeous with the best salad bar and breakfast bar. It was presented as resort style living, not assisted living."

Seniors may have aches and pains but from speaking with thousands of them over the decades, and they don't feel old, they don't want to be seen as old. Many prefer to remain living in their own homes relying on others to assist with transportation, daily chores, and care services. Many people need help with medications and other services but don't like the stigma attached to assisted livings being urine-soaked nursing homes from the 20[th]century.

Families even promise their loved ones to never place them in an institution. If it gets to the point where they decide to move into a 'retirement' independent living community then they must hire private caregivers to help when needed. Independent livings generally aren't licensed to provide care. People are supposed to be independent in independent living.

They don't want to be seen as old and no one wants to lose their independence even if they have limited mobilities, conditions and diseases like Parkinson's, a severe stroke, Alzheimer's, or substance abuse. Independent senior living communities are not regulated like assisted livings, but I see them being built almost as fast. Many elders will tell you they want to live and die in their homes. But circumstances sometimes force a move into a senior living community. Since independent living doesn't sound as bad, sometimes inappropriate people move in when they're better off in a place that has around the clock hands-on caregivers.

Since caregivers are not on the payroll for independent living communities, it's not quite as expensive to live in them. They provide meals and light-weekly housekeeping alleviating electric, trash, sewer, and other bills making it less expensive than maintaining a house. Independent living also provides socialization with other agemates so it's a great option – for people who are independent.

71

---◆---

"Of all people I had the hardest time convincing my mom to move into assisted living. I mean, I should be the best salesperson ever. It took an act of God to get her into that apartment. Mom worked until she was 87. She was never old. She said, "old people

move into assisted living and they have dances. I'm not dancing with old people!" She told the staff don't come knock on her door and say, "OK, Bingo time" because she's going to tell you to get the hell out of here, I don't play bingo. She talks on the phone and likes her own TV."

As time goes by it appears independent living is becoming the new assisted living with private caregivers, and assisted living is becoming nursing homes and geriatric behavior health facilities with unskilled workers because we are admitting residents with combative behaviors. Although assisted living was initially intended to be for people who didn't require around the clock nursing services, that's what it seems to be morphing into.

Too many people are waiting until there is a crisis to begin seeking care services; after a fall and fracture, or repeated UTIs, or after an elder has wandered away from home and gotten lost prompting a 'silver alert'. People are in denial about needing care and families are in denial about how dire the situation is for their loved ones. Until something drastic happens, adult children don't feel it's right to force their parents to move into assisted living so independent living is the compromise. Every location needs move ins and will accept just about anyone in any condition to keep their census high, not to forget salespeople get bonuses on top of salaries. But is it ethical for independent living communities to move in dementia residents, or assisted livings to move in nursing residents? Denial by one side. Denial by the other? Whatever! Come in and tour. I have four empty rooms at this moment and that ain't ok. We are offering $500 off the community fee if you take financial possession by the 30th day of this month...wink-wink, net growth, striving to 100% census.

72

———◆———

"Everyone smile there's a tour today, or make sure the resident's clothes aren't overfilling because we have a tour today, or make sure the residents look good in memory care because we have a tour today. It's all a show, none of it is genuine. Some of the caregivers have attitudes and barely even talk to each other."

Now that most people who fought in WW2 and others from the GI generation are departing, it's the Baby Boomers that are moving into senior care facilities. Some Baby-Boomers have been thinking ahead and saving for retirement. The better-off ones are paying premiums for private long-term-care insurance policies to cover fees associated with costly care services. But, as with all generations, there are many who simply aren't saving because they can't afford to, they're bad at managing money, or maybe they'd rather not think about the fact that we will all be faced with needing help eventually. That's just life. No matter our age, anyone is one accident or illness away from requiring care services.

After years of speaking with people I have come to realize so many have no idea about private Long-Term-Care insurance covering in-home caregivers, assisted living fees, and nursing facilities depending on what each person pays into. Read the fine print. Even if someone can afford private LTC insurance, once they reach around the age of 80, or if they are ill, it's likely too late to purchase a policy so best to start premiums before being diagnosed with a debilitating disease and before growing too old. I'm not promoting insurance companies, but it's important everyone has access to information that may one day cover service needs. We know everyone wants to live and die at home, that's just not possible for everyone in the new millennium.

73

"It is not going to be home, your house. It's going to be a new experience, uncomfortable when they move in because they've been used to controlling when they eat, when they play cards, when they pay bills. To a certain degree they lose control of that, but they don't have to cook anymore, we have a cook. You don't have to get up and take care of responsibilities, painting it in a different picture of we're giving you more independence, you don't have to do grocery shopping or other chores anymore. You can go on the bus with the group instead of waiting for the daughter or son to come." It's how you present it to mom versus, "You're not safe at home, we're putting you in assisted living." What that says is I'm going to lose control of everything. You gain more than you think your losing. But it's not home. It's not going to be your house, it's not where your kids grew up, a lot of times you don't have a big kitchen, there's things that you give up, but you get nutrition, you get the right medication. And if something's not right there are people around to help figure it out. If you're not feeling well, we're here to help figure out what's going on. You have advocates around where sons and daughters may not be around enough to do those things. If you think you're going to convince her this is their new home, it isn't. Doesn't look like my home, doesn't feel like my home. It will be the new normal."

Assisted living rooms and care fees cost thousands of dollars per month depending on the location and demographics of the facility, the size of rooms, and services needed by the individual resident. While Medicare is health insurance, Medicaid, or welfare, for seniors goes way beyond food stamps. Medicaid includes state-subsidized caregiving services for those who require it and meet the criteria. Some low-income seniors may receive care in their home or in an assisted living setting. Facilities must be contracted with the state to receive financial reimbursement by Medicaid for providing room and board and care services – and the facility must wait two or more months after services have been provided to receive financial reimbursement. Whatever social security or income the senior receives is usually swallowed up to offset care fees.... minus around $100 for the resident to purchase personal incidentals like toothpaste.

Not all locations care to contract with Medicaid because the reimbursement rate is a fraction of private-pay fees, that is until facilities absolutely must because of struggling with low census. If the census gets too low, they may start admitting residents on Medicaid. At that point, like my Boomer mom always said, "a little bit of something is better than a whole lot of nothing!" The shiny new pennies try desperately to remain private pay communities for as long as possible, but some are forced to give in having residents pay privately for the first year or two before they are allowed to spend-down and 'roll over' onto Medicaid. During the initial tour process, we ask lots of questions to determine if someone qualifies for different types of benefits to help cover the expensive assisted living fees. We realize many people didn't know about private LTC insurance until it was too late, and some aren't aware of benefits such as VA Aid and Attendance, and palliative care through Hospice.

Veterans and their spouses may qualify for financial assistance for personal care services, and the rest of us who are not veterans have already paid into social services that often go unused. I don't currently market for Hospice companies, but I advocate for them knowing the blessing their services are for my residents and employees in the facility. Residents and families are eased as much as possible through the stages, and employees get a little reprieve when Hospice comes in to provide showers and other comforting services.

Marketing directors pound the pavement striving to build meaningful relationships with all sorts of outside service providers with hopes to receive leads from physicians, independent livings, hospitals, rehabilitations, skilled nursing facilities, and even Hospice companies. All of them! Churches, and funeral homes, too, because widows may be contemplating a move. Healthcare facilities are looking for beds for their discharging patients that can no longer live alone and assisted living marketers are looking for residents to move in even if it's an emergency last minute situation. We'll even take short-term respite stays of 30-days or less. But what we really want are long-term residents that won't die or move out for a really long time. Every day is a $200+ day for each room so 'no lost revenue days' is the motto. The pandemic made connecting with professional discharge planners a bit complicated because we couldn't stroll inside and visit prompting us to rely more heavily on referral specialists and agencies to send us new leads. We also find new residents by hosting events and sending out invitations to lure people in and or spending a lot of money on advertising with hopes of a call or online inquiry. Lately it seems when a family goes online to seek a senior living community the link they click on goes to a national call center for referral companies. Their representatives supply you with information for facilities in the location of your interest at no charge to the family. I get emails with basic information about the lead, and I immediately contact them. Have some photos, here are the prices, please join us for a lunch tour.

74

"They move in and want to fit all their furniture and belongings from a house into a small studio apartment. One lady had so many boxes she could barely move through the room, so the executive director told her it's against fire code and she had to get rid of her stuff. I don't know why her daughter moved all that stuff into that little room."

National referral companies send inquirers a list of multiple locations, but only for the ones they're contracted with. They will also send your information to the marketers and executive directors of assisted livings who may call you persistently for years to follow. Having to work the database and call people you already harassed two months ago sucks! Yes, I'm complaining. "I told you last time I was looking for the future, maybe in a few years, no time soon. Stop calling me." That's a cold lead. If they're looking to move in 2-4 months, that's a warm lead. Withing the next 30 days, that's a hot lead and I'm going to be all over that sending cards and candy and inviting them to lunch and bingo.

I've got to keep my pipeline full, and some local referral agents help a lot with that. They usually come with the warm and hot leads so they're golden, even if they do take 100% or more of the 1ˢᵗ month's fees. That's right, over $5,000 for one assisted living referral. Whichever facility you choose to move into gets to pay a fee equivalent to the resident's first monthly payment in assisted living. We pay part of the referral fee at the time of move in, and the remainder 30-days after move in. Sometimes the resident doesn't stay or live that long, reminding everyone that some people move in at very high acuity often being on end-of-life Hospice. When Hospice or a medical facility sends us referrals, we don't have to pay fees since they are under Medicare guidelines. But referral agencies are raking in the dough. The last move-in referral-fee I paid was $7,100 to a local referral agent.

There sure are a lot of referral agents and agencies out there nowadays which leads us to senior trafficking. Some shady referring folks moved a resident into a new facility every few months to keep raking in the fees off one resident. There are other definitions and situations involved in senior trafficking but that is just one of the many ways that seniors are exploited.

75

"You've gotten to a point where you can't take care of your loved-one anymore and you brought them here to be cared for so you're going to have to trust us. If you can't trust our staff to take care of the resident, then you should consider moving them and I'm ok with that. If you can't trust us, then why are you here. Maybe this isn't the community for you. We don't want you stressing over your loved-one's care setting expectations. No, they're not going to be checked on every two minutes, it'll be more like every two hours. Your mom fell and wasn't found for fifteen minutes, that's going to happen. If you don't want that to happen, you need a 24-hour caregiver."

Years ago, my supervisor's office was across the hall from mine, and she couldn't help but laugh as the listened to me conduct a competitive marketing analysis over the phone. I made up an absurd story of how my mom and dad, a well spouse and an ill spouse, needed senior living. I had to make up the story because the marketer wasn't allowed to give their rates to a competitor. There's nothing confidential about how much care costs in this very expensive industry. The same goes for competitive payroll analysis knowing just about every assisted living pays their caregivers and medication assistants around the same hourly wage, give, or take a dollar or two.

Marketing analyses are basically contacting other assisted living and dementia care communities to compare rates, square footage of apartments, and current census, among other non-confidential things. Marketers are expected by their companies to complete competitive marketing analysis, yet their very own company may not be cooperative and won't disclose rates to other marketers needing the very same information for their own bosses. I have been told by several company's marketers and administrators, "We are not allowed to disclose our rates, but you can go on our website and get them." How dumb is that? That company posted rates on their website but wouldn't allow their marketers to disclose rates to other marketers over the phone.

Sometimes, apartment rates are so secretive they are not posted on the websites either. Most of the time I simply hung up the phone and called back a few minutes later pretending to be looking for a place for my loved one. But I must make up a name or else the company may 'kinda-sorta' own the name in the future. "I'm interested in your community. How much are your rates?" Then when they follow up weeks later, I spill the beans of confession bursting their un-bonused bubble. Guess I'm the coldest lead out there.

CHAPTER FIVE

Getting Paid To Sleep

S ome employees make poor decisions they'll have to live with for the rest of their lives. From car tires being slashed in the parking lot to employees literally following each other home with intentions of physical assault, some caregivers don't think about the fact that assault and battery is illegal. In three different facilities caregivers were slashing each other's tires and keying each other's cars. They bring their personal-life and bad attitudes to work allowing it to interfere with their ability to perform their job duties. If the phone rings asking for a caregiver I can't verify if they work in the facility because some people have stalkers.

When people call the facility looking for caregivers and other employees my radar goes off. If it's the pharmacy or a medical office calling, that's not a problem. But when it's a personal call, "Is this an emergency?" If the answer is no, "I'm not sure if that person works here but I can pass a message, or you can call them on their personal phone."

76

"I worked in a community and was at the front desk when I answered the phone. The caller asked if one of the caregivers was there and I said yes. I didn't think anything of it and that evening I went home like usual. The next day I learned the caregiver got beat up by the ex-boyfriend in the parking lot after I left. He was looking for her for weeks and I'm the one that told him where she worked. I felt so bad."

77

"Two caregivers had been quarreling about trivial matters, over who gave a shower and who didn't document it or whatever. One went up to the other who was assisting a resident and she asked for help. They argued and it turned into an all-out brawl physically fighting. The maintenance director tried to break it up. The director of nursing lost three of her fingernails. One of the caregivers had a hand full of hair in her hand having ripped it out of the other caregiver's head. There was blood and screaming. We had to separate them. One of the caregivers ran off into the parking lot and left, then later came back to give a statement. The other caregiver stayed and gave a statement. I guess a caregiver was supposed to give the shower, they didn't, and the nurse had to do it. The nurse was flipping them off, saying, "Get out! I don't *care! You're replaceable!" This would be unacceptable behavior in other industries. This was in front of the other staff members and in front of the residents in a memory care community. This was during the pandemic in 2020. They broke jewelry, broke nails, pulled out hair, all over a shower.*

Caregiving is a tough job, and everyone needs help at once. Residents are on the same meal schedule, wake and sleep schedule so everyone needs care at the same time. Caregivers that work are seen rushing from one resident to the next. And residents move slowly, and they want to tell stories while seven or more residents have already pressed their call button needing assistance. They've got catheter bags strapped to their legs that need to be emptied and ointments that need to be applied after having bowel movements which can't be rushed. Especially with those who feel like they've always got to go. Sometimes one resident presses their call button for help multiple times an hour, all day, all evening, and all morning, genuinely feeling like something's coming out. It took one lady almost 15 minutes for me to help her in the bathroom because she was sick and dizzy. I could not leave her side.

One family member is upset with me right now because she wants one of the caregivers to follow her husband around the community with a wheelchair behind as he uses a walker to strengthen his legs and get exercise. We would absolutely love to do that, but we have dozens of other residents that need their briefs changed and medications administered. There's no way we can provide a one-on-one caregiver, especially nowadays. He can barely stand, and it would take a half hour or more to follow him around. So, I advised to seek out a physical therapist and that threw her over the top. Now she's looking to move him out. I know she just wants the best for her husband, but I also know he deliberately causes problems and agitates the staff. Another family is upset because of the rate increase so now every little thing upsets them. I understand their frustrations knowing they pay $8,000 per month, but that's still much less than hiring a private caregiving company to send a one-on-one caregiver at over $20,000 per month.

I was told by the maintenance director to watch what the cameras in memory care recorded the previous night. I saw a lady with dementia sitting in her wheelchair being harassed by a caregiver sitting off to the side of her. The caregiver had a paper 'king' crown that she kept putting on the resident's head after it was clear the resident didn't want it on her head. Each time, the resident reached her hands out to stop the caregiver to no avail and I could see she was getting agitated. Then the hat fell on the ground behind the wheelchair and the caregiver got up and put her hands in the resident's face to tuck her hair behind her ear. The resident was swinging her arms trying to make her stop. The caregiver picked up the crown, and from behind the wheelchair she put the paper hat on the resident's head again. And when the resident knocked it off, she put it on her head again, physically, and psychologically bullying this poor demented little old 85, maybe 90-pound helpless lady.

I can't imagine what it's like losing my mental faculties, mobility, or having to give up my independence. It's a lot different to work in assisted living than to live in one. Although some people absolutely love not having to cook and clean anymore, there are people who openly express their grief. A colleague of mine turned me on to a YouTube video that really made many people in the industry reconsider the culture and become stronger advocates for change. The 20 or so minute video is called "The Thin Edge of Dignity" where an assisted living resident literally tells us how he feels and what's it like living in an assisted living facility. He spoke of being called a number to maintain HIPPA confidentiality practices and feeling helpless to do the once easy task of grasping a glass of water. Dependent on others for care, living on the thin edge of dignity. The short video is worth the watch.

78

"There was resident trapped inside of two chairs put together and it looked like a crib. Confined and physically restrained, trying to crawl out, the employees took cushions out of the bottom of the chairs so it was deeper. The husband wanted her that way to prevent her from falling and executive director thought it was a good idea. They put her near in the front entrance so staff could see her. Then it was a recliner with legs up, still confined, and unable to get up to prevent her from falling. This is assisted living; we can't do that. The regional nurse didn't care because she didn't want falls and lawsuits but wanted to maintain census. She now has physical therapy and even though she's still a two person assist we have a confinement waver.

79

"As the executive director I'm constantly talking people off the ledge, families that are running out of money, what do we do? They're mad at me even though they aren't. You're a counselor, you're everything, a social worker, educator, I have to be a cook, a caregiver. We go out of our way to the brink of exhaustion but are met by ungrateful families and residents. It is so hard to win the game when some of your team is sitting in the grass while the cheerleaders are constantly picking you apart.

80

"They'd wait until I left, and they were the most rude, intimidating people. If they thought I wasn't in the building they would come in and harass the caregivers about, "Look at this on the floor, "Why isn't that clean, where is this, why didn't you do this?" And the caregivers would run! There wasn't a caregiver in sight because they were hiding. Every time they walked in something isn't right. They were trying to play the advocate role, but it was about power and intimidation. And that was a preacher."

Built on sacred burial ground, or whatever the case may be, I have now worked in numerous communities in crisis in different states that were all struggling with the very same problems. I know of many more problem communities from touring them and having colleagues working in them that complained of the same issues. As a regional, I have personally hired dozens of caregivers over a two-month period and most of them didn't show up to their first day of orientation. The ones that did show up only worked for a few days then quit. Some interviewees were job hoppers, bouncing to a new facility every few months. Others were mature, career minded and had stable employment at one company for multiple years seeking a career change. Regardless of how well they presented themselves in the interview, we were desperate, and most quit before their 30[th]day.One applicant said she had to satisfy the government enough to ensure she would still receive food stamps and cash assistance. She gets free medical care and here I am paying hundreds of dollars each month for health insurance. Without getting too political, I often wonder why welfare isn't designed to offer a temporary helping hand instead of enabling able bodied 'would be' workers to receive handouts year after year. Over the years I have asked employees their thoughts and many said they don't like to work and only do so when they must. But they would work if it were their own business.

Whether or not it has to do with welfare, there are just not enough workers to care for the residents in challenged communities. It's not like all interviews were with youngsters wearing cutoff jeans and t-shirts. Yes, I did conduct a fair number of interviews with unprofessional millennials up to middle aged folks, all of whom were dismissed for obvious reasons. But many of the applicants either had extensive caregiving experience and knew what the job entailed, or they had work experience in other fields like fast food and construction making it their very first time working in healthcare. So, I had to explain in detail what the job entailed. That way, there was no mistake that they would be changing the diapers of 200lb grown men and women, and physically washing naked elder bodies in the shower.

I can recall one new hire who I thought would eventually advance to become a manager from her experience and confident attitude during the interview. The orientation process was just about as it is in other locations; shadowing other new caregivers because everyone seems to be new, and of course the caregivers try to do as little work as possible. After only a few days of working, she quit and filed a neglect complaint with the state. But she sat on her butt playing on her phone most of the night, just like the other caregivers that she complained about. In my experience most caregivers want the night shift to be paid for sleeping.

81

————◆————

"*It must have been just before midnight when I randomly checked the cameras and saw the caregivers getting all cozy on the couch about to watch a movie, bowls of popcorn in hand. I started talking into the microphone, "Does anyone want to tell me what's going on?" They looked around wondering where the sound was coming from, wondering if it came from the television. So, I said, "This is your boss. What is going on? I'm not paying you to watch movies."*

Since there is so much turnover, the new employees are training newer employees...basically the blind leading the blind. This is part of the reason why we can't retain caregivers. Management is spread too thin to jump into an hour of training. They can't dedicate a full day or more to it. In some locations employees start orienting and training on different days so it takes up a lot of time. Managers keep turning over, so systems put in place to prevent critical errors break down or are disregarded all together. The stellar new caregivers with positive attitudes who at first said they'd work double shifts, 16-hour days, are overworked and scheduled seven days a week for a month straight without a day off. Then the good employees quit due to burnout leaving nurses and administrators scrambling, caregiving and passing medications on graveyard shifts.

82

"The last time I almost walked out I called the executive director and asked for help because I was taking care of all the residents by myself. No one else showed up to work that day. A few hours later she came in with her young daughter holding a plate of cookies and said, "we baked these for you." She handed me the cookies and left a short time later. She did not help. I didn't eat them, I and just left the cookies on her desk."

83

"Call lights can go unanswered up to 15 or 30 minutes. When you have a memory care or assisted living that has 20, 60, 100 residents, your expectation that a resident pushes their call light, and a caregiver responds within a ten-minute period may be unrealistic. Unfortunately, we're looking at the number of caregivers which we are already lacking, and the high acuity of 30 or 40 incontinent people who all need attention. And there's the lack of urgency from the caregivers. You've got caregivers who are tired, who work two and three jobs. And some residents in memory care can't remember to press their call lights. Ten minutes is about average, and it's not going to happen right away"

What happens when administrators work as caregivers at night? There is no management around during normal business hours. When the cat is away, the mice oversee the community. Of course, the constant mess is blamed on the current executive director that eventually quits or gets fired and replaced with someone who struggles to control the chaos. The new ultimately runs on the same squeaky hamster wheel that's loud enough to summon the state agencies in, again. Additional resources are temporarily sent to the community such as regional operations directors and regional nurses only to continue the interview process and potentially work graveyard shifts themselves. Ok, that was a joke because 99% of regionals are not working graveyard shifts. But it also appears that 99% of caregivers that work the night shift do so to get paid for sleeping. Most are there just to have a warm body at night.

In a perfect world, on-boarding and training new caregivers should be a no brainer. Every state has its own requirements, and every company has its own policies, none of which seem to be known by anyone other than the executive director. Many times, the problem comes down to communities hiring out of desperation, so steps get missed or people don't have current CPR and 1st AID or whatever but get put on the schedule because we need bodies working on the floor. Thorough orientation and training are rare in assisted living facilities, and so are 30- or 90-day follow-ups to see how employees like their new job. Most don't last 30-90 days. There should be a process in place to maintain the new hire's job description, offer letter and other necessary documents so they are not misplaced. There should also be a process where all new hire documents that need to be filled out are easy to find so nothing gets forgotten. A new hire should not have to fill out forgotten documents weeks after beginning, that's if they're still employed there which is usually is not the case.

If the new hire will be working as a caregiver, it's in the best interest of the community for the person to receive training on all shifts so they understand the duties of other caregivers and get to know the residents' personalities. It's most important if they're being hired on as an overnight caregiver. Care services training should incorporate items such as how to approach, interact and engage with residents, redirecting residents, bathing, dressing, grooming, changing, and transferring residents. And nowadays since people are waiting longer to move in, coming with higher acuity, training on how to operate Hoyer lifts, how to care drain catheters, and training on other medical services is needed.

New hires should learn where to locate care plans and how to understand and implement them, in addition to when, how and where to document services provided. Three days of training totaling 21 hours is not sufficient to expect the new hire is ok to be left alone to care for multiple residents whom they barely know. And after 21 hours of training, they likely haven't retained information regarding what to do if the fire alarm sounds or a resident goes missing. They're passing medications before they're properly trained to do so. Companies spend thousands of dollars recruiting new employees, interviewing, hiring, screening, onboarding, and training people with high chances of quitting almost right away due to low pay and a stressful work environment which is stressing managers to the core.

84

"The whole drawer was filled with pre-poured medications for the day, and they know better they just got away with it for so long. They don't care about the training, we go over things at shift change and they don't care, they just won't do their jobs correctly. It's the biggest fight we have. And they want me to reward them and buy them lunch."

Caregivers wouldn't work in the facility if they didn't have some sense of compassion and patience. They wouldn't work for low wages doing the challenging job if there weren't something enticing them to remain in the field. For all the physical, mental, and emotional abuse caregivers endure from upset residents, families, co-workers, and supervisors, most of them tend to be career caregivers even if they don't continue working in that facility. Often, caregivers float from place to place which means there is a constant revolving door in locations with heavy competition. This is not always the fault of management; it tends to be the case much of the time.

Managers must deal with gossipers and nasty attitudes run good caregivers away. There's a saying, "people don't quit jobs, they quit bosses." Well, I have learned caregivers have an endless number of reasons and excuses why they quit, and it doesn't always have anything to do with management. I do all I can to be a leader and a manager that employees can openly talk to and feel comfortable around. But I too have been left scrambling to find last minute replacements for last-minute call off and no-shows. Caregivers constantly want time off, or they call off or just flat out quit without any notice. They talk all that mess about 'being here for the residents' yet they will leave the residents hanging without anyone to provide care. It's cold hearted, for sure.

I get call offs for weekends all the time and some of the call-off excuses are questionable. Caregivers are responsible for covering their own shifts if they must call off, but there are usually not enough caregivers employed at the facility or no one answers their phone so they can't find coverage. If the caregiver can't find coverage, they tend to call off anyways and then I must figure out coverage.

85

"*I can't come to work. There are all these excuses. She just wanted the day off. You try to be as compassionate and understanding, even before it was cool. We've always had to be flexible. You don't have day care, you don't have a babysitter, you're a single mom, this isn't just a new COVID thing. Can you come in for half a shift, can we pick you up, I've picked up people in the snow, 4w drives, even a blizzard.*"

86

"*Staffing had always been a challenge. And there's a problem with the fact that we can fire a caregiver for abuse or neglect but there's nowhere* to report them in this state, so they simply begin working at another *community. We have more people coming in that are not qualified or not willing to do their job. It used to be that we had some staff members that had been there for ten years, or fifteen years. But as time has gone by it has become more and more challenging to retain people. Now it's more like ten months, and it has slowly gotten to the point that if a caregiver has stayed with the company for six months, then that's a long time. And trying to find caregiving staff now is near impossible. They came with the premise that we have one of the largest retirement centers in the U. S., so Florida, Arizona are two states that have large populations of 65 and older. All these companies came and built so you've got companies that saw an opportunity and started building five and six locations here and there. They were waiting* on the big wave of Baby boomers. But they didn't take staffing into consideration."

"We do not have this caliber of staffing with the rate of pay that they want to give. Back in the day beginning wages were $9, $10 an hour, let's say between 2005 and 2010. Rates went up in small increments after that to $12.50 and $13 an hour. Then we hit 2020 and all the communities were desperately trying to share a shrinking pool of caregivers and the bottom fell out. Not only were we requiring them to do their job, but the caregivers were getting sick with COVID. They were beginning to question whether they would make more money if they weren't working because of the incentives that came from the government. And they started rethinking whether they wanted to be in this field because it's difficult. It's hard, the work is incredibly physical especially in memory care and assisted living population where you have to do two-person assists. And there's only one worker there. The medication management is becoming more of a challenge because more people are sicker on more medications. And behaviors were happening because of COVID. The behaviors of people with dementia became worse with the lack of socialization. The families could no longer visit or take their loved one's out to help quell some of the behaviors. Now you've got the perfect storm. You've got behaviors, high acuity levels, more medications, and no staffing."

Just above minimum wage is the standard pay for caregivers who, most of the time, don't have enough gas money to make it to their next paycheck, let alone enough money to pay their bills. Inflation is high, caregivers have kids to feed and it's impossible to live comfortably on several hundred dollars per week. Many caregivers are working multiple jobs and picking up as much overtime as possible just to survive. And they are not allowed to receive tips. Recently the minimum wage increased in several states and the COVID-19 pandemic made people question their career choices. Many senior care companies were forced to increase caregiver's wages which messes with the investor's profits resulting in an increase in assisted living fees.

"Just put me on the schedule to work doubles every day." A common phrase of caregivers requesting to work 16 hour shifts 5 or more days per week. Then, burnout. In this scenario, when the caregiver who is scheduled to work two shifts each day back-to-back calls off or gets sick from overwork and stress it's left to the supervisor to replace both shifts with other employees who are also exhausted from overwork. Recently I did an interview with a caregiver that said she wanted full time overnight shifts Monday through Thursday. She said she already had another job but needed more hours because she couldn't afford her bills anymore. She was so tired that sometimes she didn't make any sense when she talked about her availability. I told her to write down when she can work, and she said she wasn't sure anymore and would call me when she figures it out.

The grass appears greener on the other side of the fence where facility B is offering caregivers five cents more an hour, so the caregiver quits and gets hired on over there only to realize they're up the same creek; still underpaid and grossly overworked. How many hours in a day or week can one human being work and still have enough travel time to and from, sleep time, personal time, and family time. The latter is non-existent, and the sleep is compromised. In multiple locations I have regularly processed paychecks for employees who worked 160 or more hours in a two-week pay period. We can't care for residents if we don't have caregivers. Caregivers are the backbone of any assisted living yet were sometimes paid less than the housekeepers before the pandemic. It's not a secret why it's challenging to retain caregivers.

For so many of us working in assisted living, scheduling is the worst job to have. It's really time consuming and the schedule is way too fluid. Even some of the best caregivers have emergencies pop up. There are all sorts of legitimate reasons such as an illness of a child or themselves, a death in the family, and other issues that justify a last-minute request off. But, we all know, most of the time the day off requests is because they're burning out and need to sleep or just want to have some fun in life or family time. Low paid caregivers are already stealing away too much time from their personal lives just to survive until the next paycheck, and many of them are working doubles because they can't afford not to. There simply aren't enough good caregivers employed, and the burnt-out ones are too tired to pick up another shift. Half the time caregivers wait until the very last minute to call off if they call off at all, or they become ghosts not answering our phone calls or text messages.

87

"*I would literally spend hours on the schedule, why is this so hard? 5 caregivers in the morning, 5 caregivers in the evening, and 3 caregivers overnight for 40 residents: my labor budget is good. I'm under hours each month, we just can't find caregivers. 12-hour shifts are really hard because if someone calls off, the last person can't work 24-hours straight. We use agency, everyone wants 6-2 M-F. I struggle with nights and weekends. Me, my nurse, and another manager rotate manager on duty. And when I gave my 30-day notice they never called me, they never thanked me for all I had done over the years.*"

 # 88

---◆---

"In 9 months, I've spent around $2000 of my own money. At first, I did raffles, and I did TVs and nice things. And two caregivers said "I would cover the shift but you're not giving away TVs anymore so I'm not coming in." I was trying to be nice and now they expect it. We're still using agency.

Schedules should be posted well in advance because not everyone always gets the very same schedule every single week. Yes, there are some who are inflexible, demanding their schedule be consistent or they'll quit. This is in some ways good. The posted schedule is always changing which causes terrible confusion and people not showing up to care for residents putting extra pressure on the caregivers that did. In some cases, a caregiver's schedule will change, and they won't even be asked or notified. Just because the schedule is posted doesn't mean that's what it will look like after the month is over, or even after the week for that matter. It's just so fluid with all the call offs. There are many instances of facilities that have only one caregiver for 30 – 40 people, and some locations are going without. Facilities are trying to hire. Hourly rates are going up from $12 per hour up over $20. I know this because some of our caregivers left to go to our competitor and we're paying $20 per hour. There are bonuses being given, several hundred for caregivers, several thousand for nurses. And we're competing against hospitals that offer sign on bonuses of tens of thousands of dollars.

89

"*I commend caregivers, they have a hard job, but with the competition they just jump from place to place. And we're so desperate that we need to fill the position that they get hired back even after they've walked off the job. We are so desperate, we're giving bonuses, but they continue to misuse us. If we give them any feedback or coaching, they'll just be like, "no, I'm not going to do it that way" and they'll just walk off.*

90

"*I feel like the caregivers are ruling the industry right now, they rule my building. Two weekends ago paid someone $200 to come to work because she said she doesn't have any gas, and that was her normally scheduled shift. Brand new caregiver, first week on the job and she called off. "Why doesn't your community offer gas money to your caregivers?" $17-19 for caregivers, $20-22 for med techs ...five years ago they were making $4-5 an hour less than that. And they know because they've worked in this industry for years. And now they want gas money on top of that, and they'll negotiate with you. "I'll do it for $50," or they'll ask, "will you buy us lunch because we got all our ADLs done." That's your job, are you kidding me right now. They weren't even charting. ...sometimes I think they work just enough to cover their bills then they're like, now I've had enough, and they call off. They do have a hard job, but our reward is our paycheck. Do you think I could call the owner of our management company and tell them I will* *come to work if they give me gas money? That's not happening. I'm so desperate for caregivers that me and my nurse went in on it together with money from our own pockets, just to have the shift covered so we don't have to come in again."*

91

"They need money, they need reward, they need praise. Staff frustrates me. It's more than residents and families, everyday it's crazy weird things the staff does. Every week someone has something wrong in their personal lives. I give compassion and they take advantage of me.

Assisted living is not alone in the struggle since medical home health companies, in-home-care companies, hospitals, rehabs, skilled nursing, and other facilities are in desperation for workers to accommodate the constant need. Several of the assisted living facilities I know of are utilizing in-home care companies and nurse registries to fill open shifts in their assisted livings because there aren't enough workers. But they're all short staffed, too. With how bad it is today; I can't imagine the desperation our country will be in within the next two decades knowing dementia will increase. It's a harsh reality to face; if you don't currently know someone in your inner circle that has serious vascular and circulation problems or a diagnosis of dementia, you likely will in the near future. It's in our best interest to reconstruct senior care in our county. Even if by then we have enough senior care facilities to accommodate the growing need, caregivers aren't lining up to change adult briefs and get beat up while trying to redirect combative behaviors at poverty wages.

92

———◆———

"It's a lot of responsibility with zero oversight by an RN. It's way too much for an LPN and it opens us up to litigation. It's scary. At one point we didn't have any true oversight by an RN, and I always felt bad for the LPNs. It was best to have RNs especially in memory care. The best director I had was a social worker because she was working with the resources for the families and counseling the families, it wasn't as much clinical as it was emotional. So, memory care really is emotion, activities, social work and of course meeting the residents care needs. But it seems the need is more with the families and walking the journey with them. Sometimes nurses look at a behavior and a med instead of looking at the relationship between the mother and the visiting daughter. We overlook why does she get combative? We don't know their history and how their relationship was. Memory care was like a puzzle because you had to figure out who goes where, and why. Someone shows up and this behavior happens, and that person responds like this, and it's all emotion, tough emotion. We just love a certain family member, but we don't know the back story. Sometime there's decades of resentment and guilt. Stories are playing out 40 years later and sometimes the residents are living in the past. Trying to fit all those pieces together.

Dementia is a hot topic nowadays but there is still much confusion around it - Pun intended - I've got to make light in this book somehow. Unfortunately, there's way too much old-school lingo and thinking around dementia, in general. Calling facilities 'Memory Care' is one of the problems since many people with dementia don't have severe memory loss. I have met many people with vascular dementia from a stroke that remembered a lot. Even my grandfather who had Parkinson's dementia didn't suffer from severe memory loss until the very end of his disease process. But my grandmother who had Alzheimer's disease; Yes, severe memory loss there. We still have so much to learn since over 100 conditions cause dementia, but people keep calling it 'All-timers' or 'old-timers'. I don't think there is a disease called All-timers. And Alzheimer's disease is not dementia, it causes dementia. Dementia is an umbrella term for the group of neuro-degenerative symptoms of severe cognitive decline.

Anyways, then we have the large and fancy 20th century / last millennium style assisted livings with dedicated dementia care units being built all over the country. Some companies are building dementia friendly villages with cafes and theaters, and all sorts of new hybrid communities are shifting the paradigm. We're all familiar with the large and spread-out fancy locations. There are also medium sized cottages that house around a dozen people. I like how people in the similar stages of dementia are grouped together so early stage isn't with end of life. But that set up poses staffing challenges on top of the already problematic staffing shortage. In the cottage set up caregivers are scheduled to work in each cottage overnight with a medication assistant that floats through. It would be great if caregivers were reliable.

93

"One evening a family members went into check on her loved one. The floating caregiver let her into the secured community allowing her to visit her husband. But when the visitor was ready to leave there weren't any employees around. She rang and called for assistance to get out and no one ever came. Not one caregiver was in that cottage for the entire night. No one came to check on

the residents and she was forced to sleep in the facility that night. This story came to me directly from that family member. The family took their loved one out and sued the company. The visitor was trapped in the facility all night because no one was around to let her out."

94

"A caregiver complained to me, "I'm not getting my hours." Well stop calling off and have a consistent schedule. When we need coverage! Pick up the shift."

It's uncommon for one caregiver to work a 'straight through' 24-hour shift in an assisted living facility. But it does happen more that I'd care to admit because if no one shows up, the caregiver cannot abandon the residents and leave them all alone. These are the caregivers who are in it for the right reasons, but everyone has their breaking point. A good caregiver functioning on little to no sleep continuously will, well, fall asleep. What good is a sleepy caregiver who is supposed to care for dozens of residents? Lifting and transferring a 100 pound to 300-pound resident from a wheelchair to the toilet, then back again after providing intimate care services takes more than just strength and skill, but also, focus. I mean, let's face it; it's one thing to work in a retail store and drop a T-shirt, but potentially a broken hip or fractured skull and an accusation of abuse or neglect if a caregiver drops a frail, elderly resident. "I've been working 16-hour shifts for two weeks straight without a day off" is not an acceptable excuse to emergency first responders, families or the state agency investigating the family's complaint. Unfortunately, some assisted living facilities and group homes have caregivers that got in their cars and left the residents all alone when their replacement didn't show up. No one showed up so the caregiver just left. That is neglect. Neglect happens all the time and it's not being reported. Healthcare workers are mandatory reporters. But we'd be reporting people all day long every single day across this nation if we really held true to the mandate.

95

"Smokey-Tokey was in my first community. She weighed about 12 pounds because she only drank soda and smoked cigarettes. She was from the east coast, and she was on smoke breaks constantly. I got to know her because she was reliable. The younger ones were not. When I started a bunch of the smokey-tokeys ended up leaving when we cut down on smoke breaks. We offered smoking cessation. They had a smoke room, an empty room that was so gross and so yellow that we couldn't even paint over it. The residents could smell it and the smoke was through the whole hallway.

We had to buy gallons of Febreze, and the only fan was like a bathroom fan. It was supposed to be a smoke room for the residents back in the day. We were making changes and said you can't take 25 smoke breaks and the caregiver pulls out a cigarette and said, "I'm gonna tell you something, I'm not doing any of this. I've been working here for years, and this is what I'm gonna continue to do." And my director of nursing said, you're gonna do this or you're not gonna be working here. She was a good caregiver, but she followed the smokey-tokeys."

96

"I got a call at 3 o'clock in the morning. "OMG we've had a break in. A guy came in with a knife and wanted narcotics." I felt so bad for the med tech and I'm on the phone with the police. They called me back and determined the window was busted from the inside. The med tech and her boyfriend were stealing the resident's medications."

97

"The med tech was replacing a resident's narcotic with a malaria pill. It was all over the news. The resident kept getting sicker and sicker until the truth of what was happening came out.

Another caregiver was writing a list, trying to remember the narcotics she gave the previous night because she didn't document when she gave them. It was 6 AM shift change, and she left. When the executive director called her to find out what happened, the caregiver said she destroyed a resident's medications but then she confessed that she actually had a resident's medications in her pocket. She got fired but a couple of days later she was applying at a different facility."

98

"I received a new admission from out of state, so my nurse and I were unable to physically lay eyes on her prior to arrival in the facility. She was an appropriate admission, but the discharging facility only sent her with 24 hours of insulin and other life sustaining medications. She had no prescriptions or refills with her and since she was new to the state, she didn't have a local physician yet. My nurse called the out-of-state nurse practitioner for an immediate prescription of insulin so we could at very least keep her blood sugar under control. The cold-hearted nurse practitioner got rude over the phone and refused to do anything more for the patient she once 'supposedly' cared for.

My new admission should be on Hospice services, but the family is totally against it because they don't want the 'life sustaining' medications and treatments to stop. The family is in denial thinking their 88-year-old mother with COPD should have physical therapy, but she is in bad health, she is incontinent, and can only bear weight on one leg. I don't have enough caregivers as it is so at least Hospice comes in to give baths and comfort care a few of times a week to many of my residents. We need all the help we can get, and just because someone signs up for Hospice doesn't mean they're going to die any sooner. I only accepted the move in as a short-term respite stay since the family is in denial and I don't want anyone in my community to die unless they're on Hospice services. That's always a tough conversation to have with families but people need to understand that Hospice can help; it's covered under Medicare Part B, so is the hospital bed, Hoyer lift, Adult Briefs and personal wipes and gloves, oxygen therapy, and other durable medical equipment...all at no cost to the patient. Or they can spend several thousand dollars on a hospital bed and incontinence supplies wherever they decide to move to because she can't stay here. It's sad too since she's a nice resident, this is a nice facility, and she has already made friends.

CHAPTER SIX

Worst Case Scenario

On my first day as the new executive director of Heaven Forbid Senior Living one of the residents introduced himself and wanted me to be aware he had been recently physically assaulted by a homeless person. The resident is a smoker and obeys the rules of smoking outside in the designated area. Late one night as he attempted to enter the side door of the facility a homeless person ambushed, and sucker punched him causing him to fall off his electric wheelchair. The homeless person entered the building and was found the next morning sleeping in an office.

I know a police report was filed because as I left on my first evening I was met by the investigating officer. "You guys should really have a security guard in this neighborhood". Without even seeing the budget I already knew we couldn't afford a security guard. There were only 70 rooms filled in a building that had 150.

The facility was subsidized by Medicaid so the reimbursement was a fraction of what it would be if residents were paying privately.

I was no stranger to the facility that I call Heaven Forbid Senior Living, so I knew it was challenged back in the days when I first walked through the doors for networking purposes. This was simply the first time working in it, and I happened to come in as the executive director post COVID-19's fire trail which meant staff and residents freaking out about changes they knew I was going to make. Yes, I came in as the bad guy expecting low paid employees to work instead of sitting around chatting and scrolling social media.

This location was not my first rodeo. The Ghost Town in the dusty desert was. Over the years I have managed multiple locations and even trained managers for previous companies. I keep my door open and try to be easy to talk to but I'm not perfect by any means. I come in every single day smiling with a positive attitude and a lot of driving force, a whirlwind to complacency. Mostly everyone knows when I am on the compound because I work hard striving for top-notch operations, quality care, state compliance, and I ensure people are trained and held accountable for their actions. But accountability was a new phenomenon at Heaven Forbid Assisted Living. And within a few days I could tell the sloth paced staff were counting the days, waiting to see how long I will be there. 'How long is this executive director going to last' because they know people come and go in senior living, and especially in that facility which must've been built on sacred burial ground or something because it was an awful situation for the residents to live in.

I was deep into writing this book when I started working at Heaven Forbid Senior Living having already interviewed a few dozen industry professionals and written down many of my own experiences on computer-paper. I didn't anticipate adding to the work which still needed to be formatted. But since my first day as executive director unfolded more than red flags, yet the facility only got minor slaps on the wrist by regulators, I began speaking into my phone before and after work to record 'it happened today' firsthand experiences instead of strictly pulling from memories and interviews acquired over the years. So here are my voice recordings...just remember...Not all assisted living facilities are worst case scenarios like Heaven Forbid which is PBS documentary criteria all by itself.

Day 1

---◆---

"At least a half dozen residents came up to me at different times of the day saying they're not receiving meals and I noticed food being delivered to the front desk twice, but I thought it was for staff lunches. Another resident showed me pictures of their overflowing garbage can in their room and said no one will take out the trash and no one will help me take showers. I've uncovered falsified documents and medical charts that are missing practically everything including doctor's orders, and the documents couldn't be located on the electronic chart. The charts that have full code written on them but signed DNRs (Do Not Resuscitate) inside of them, and vice-versa. There aren't service plans for most residents. We don't have a nurse, but we have a caregiver who used to be a CNA years ago that pretends to be a nurse. We've got serious deficiencies in care services overall. We've got staffing shortages on every shift for every single day this week and the schedule doesn't have all the caregiver's names listed. There are also terminated caregiver's names assigned to shifts, and we've got bed bugs in more than a dozen rooms on opposite ends of the building and on different floors in the facility. And I was just met by a police investigator about a physical assault against a resident that happened in December. Some of the kitchen crew walked out last month after adult protective services got a complaint about the food being slop so the state licensing agency came out to survey. But they only found a few minor citations, so my new company is paying the fines. And the residents and staff are upset with my new dietary manager that is neither warm nor fuzzy." End of Day 1 Phone Narration

Day 2

———◆———

I learned there is a pending lawsuit regarding a resident that died. I also learned the staff have been told not to call 911 if a resident falls. Instead, call the medication technician who will access and help the resident off the floor. This is a problem since med techs don't have Xray vision to determine if there are fractures or breaks. I will conduct caregiver trainings on all shifts over the next week to ensure every caregiver is trained on 'When in Doubt - Send Them Out!' in addition to trainings on verbal, emotional and physical abuse, resident rights, and caregiver job expectations such as taking out the garbage and assisting residents with getting ready each morning." End Day 2 Phone Narration

Day 3

———◆———

"You know the saying, "I can't make this up." It's worse than the one I was at three years ago and I thought that place was bad. Adult Protective Services called me regarding a complaint about a cockroach infestation, but they didn't say anything about the footlong rats one of which I personally had to remove from a resident's room last night. Just after shift change at around 10:30 I was conducting the meeting for 3rd shift and a med tech came to me panicked stating a resident pressed their emergency pendant screaming for help. A huge rat was caught in one of the many traps that are strategically placed around the resident's room. No kidding, the rat was almost a foot long, not including the pinky thick tail, flipping, and flopping with its head stuck. Two packing boxes made it an empty scoop up. As I walked through the side door headed to the dumpster a fire truck was pulling up for a resident fall. There were people digging in the dumpster, so I told them they had to leave. Then I realized how dark the parking lot is at night, and all the lights that are out. End Day 3 Phone Narration.

This place didn't fall apart over night, and someone must be blamed for the accumulation of problems but it's not going be corporate. It doesn't matter the reason, whatever the problem in an assisted living facility, it's the manager's fault. Often the facility manager is the scapegoat for cutting costs, putting profits over people to satisfy 'corporate' or else they risk losing their jobs. Business is business, either look the other way or speak up and be another notch on the totem pole. Why else would there be dozens of roaches crawling everywhere in the kitchen and in resident rooms versus having pest control services come as often as needed? It doesn't take a rocket scientist to get pest control out here, but it costs money. It's so bad I'm surprised the facility hasn't crawled away. There are dead flies in the window seals. And no one notices, not even the health department? Look the other way because it's a Medicaid building so the residents don't deserve better? And this is just one location.

I got very familiar with dealing with bed bugs at Whispering Winds, the first assisted living where I worked many years ago. It also had rats, scabies outbreaks, and a German cockroach infestation. But I don't remember the infestations being as bad as it is at this location. I remember seeing a roach here and there, but not everywhere. And I saw the rat droppings, even heard rats in the ceilings, but I never saw one over the years. I'm seeing them all the time here. Anyways, I had pest control come with the bed bug sniffing dog then exterminate that room and all the rooms around above and beside it - so they don't find respite next door.

Bed bugs get into facilities from visitors or employees or from residents who go out on the town then return with them on their shoes or clothes. They don't spell 'filth' to me, they're hitchhikers. But we shouldn't be able to see dozens of fat adult-sized bed bugs crawling on residents and their furniture. I mean really. One of the caregivers was picking bugs off a resident that refuses to leave her room. And hordes of cockroaches and rats running throughout the building, this is absolutely disgusting, and I feel bad that the residents have been living under these terrible conditions for so long. I feel even worse about the fact that the state knows, the owners know, the employees know, the managers know, even the outside service providers know. The residents and families keep complaining. Yet no one has cared enough to make this place better.

Day 4

———◆———

At least my nurse candidate accepted the job offer and will begin next week because I just learned TB (Tuberculosis) tests were being read, and likely administered, by the caregiver who is kind of like the nurse, she thinks she's a nurse, and has the title that our new nurse is supposed to have. And I just learned she is financially compensated as the nurse because a previous executive director is her best friend and hired her at a high pay rate five years ago. She's a caregiver being paid as a nurse that refuses to fill in any caregiving shifts. She strolls in at around 10:00 AM and leaves around 2 or 3:00 PM after a long day of hanging out behind closed doors with other tenured staff. And yet caregivers doing the heavy lifting haven't gotten raises in years, if ever. Some caregivers are working here for $12.50 per hour. And here we have Pretender making a nurse's wage but doing little to nothing.

Now Pretender has hurt feelings because she doesn't want to lose the wellness director title that belongs to the nurse I just hired. She doesn't want to be called an assistant to the new nurse having already been employed at Heaven Forbid Assisted Living for so many years outlasting a dozen nurses in half a dozen years. Yes, you read that right, 12 nurses in 6 years. Pretender is a nice lady, but she's not a nurse. None of the tenured caregivers respect her or even answer her requests. That may be since she's hardly ever around, she shoots the breeze when she is here, and she comes to work in raggedy-holey jeans, spaghetti-strap shirts, and flip flops. Where's the pride for this business? Assisted living is a business but there has been absolutely no accountability. The decay of this location started way before the COVID-19 pandemic. In the dozen years of knowing Heaven Forbid Assisted Living there was no way to expect this elixir:

- a poorly managed community of many years that holds no one accountable,

- slop being passed off as food prepared in a filthy kitchen home to roaches, rodents, flies, and maggots,

- only half of the residents receiving food each day - half portions served in Styrofoam boxes,

- the Styrofoam boxes of food sit on a rolling cart for over an hour so it's cold and late by the time it's carted to residents in memory care, then eventually other residents in assisted living,

- a caregiver to resident ratio average of around 1-20 with intimate services provided by caregivers that hang out on the 4th floor couch gossiping instead of working,

- medical services overseen by a pretend nurse having already burned through 12 licensed nurses in 6 years,

- notorious for accepting inappropriate and high acuity bariatric (obese) and bedridden residents to maintain high census,

- impacted by COVID-19 which caused the census to plunge resulting in layoffs but instead incurring massive overtime and more employee burnout,

- cooped-up depressed residents still on lock down and only half of them fully vaccinated and wearing masks,

- residents sitting and laying in their rooms in their own filth that haven't been cleaned with garbage cans that overflow of rotting food,

- a bed bug infestation so terrible that a caregiver was brushing them off a demented old woman that sat in a repulsive chair,

- a rat infestation so aggressive that one crawled up a resident's pant leg as she sat in her recliner and another jumped at an employee,

- a roach infestation so sickening that simply dropping a rolling-bucket from under the dishwasher spawned a disturbing groundcover of movement,

- slated as a low-income facility so 'corporate' doesn't think the residents deserve decent living conditions like weekly pest control services to combat the multiple infestations,

- surrounded by heaps of overflowing garbage in dumpsters, cooking, baking, rotting in 110-degree summer heat,

- in a neighborhood riddled with illegal street drugs, shopping carts, make-shift tents, and homeless of which some of the residents used to be, and many of their visitors still are,

- with residents smoking weed and crystal meth and shooting up heroin in their assisted living rooms.

I have got my work cut out for me. Everyone was miserable there, and they made it known to me on my first day. I gave the green light to open the front doors since COVID-19 was starting to subside, and residents are allowed to have visitors in personal apartments for up to 60 minutes while maintaining social distancing, wearing masks, and practicing proper hand hygiene. Time to break out the dishes because we can reopen the dining room and purge all the 'to-go' boxes that are overflowing the garbage receptacles creating more pestilence. "Where are the dishes?"

The new dietary manager that started two weeks before I did just told me the dishes got thrown out by the last executive director who only lasted a few months. He also enlightened me to all the dining room chairs having been thrown away. "Everything but the tables were tossed." I could only imagine how disgusting those chairs must have been. As for the plates, what was wrong with those? Couldn't they just be washed?

Complaints about the Dietary Manager began on my very 1ˢᵗday by his own kitchen crew and by residents who told me, "That man is no chef." At first, I thought they're not even giving this guy a chance. They have no idea how filthy that kitchen really is, and I see him back there trying to clean it. The food will never look appealing and remain hot in to go boxes carted around to 100 rooms three times a day? But I am realizing there's more to it. The dietary manager has a cold shoulder, and he doesn't listen to the residents. "I have a culinary degree and worked in five-star restaurants, so I can't hear you," is his attitude so I don't foresee him lasting too long. Especially since he seems to despise training the skeleton kitchen crew that reports directly to him.

One of the cooks is in desperate need of training. Or he just needs to go all together since it's apparent he's allergic to cleaning and his appearance and food presentation is sloppy. When I heard about the 'slop' complaint I immediately imagined him. It appears we need an entirely new kitchen crew since the dietary manager doesn't listen, and 'Sloppy' doesn't clean or care about anything other than taking naps. I caught Sloppy sleeping in the resident's donated massage chair when he was supposed to be cleaning the cockroach infested kitchen or preparing dinner. After I asked him to get to work, I was informed he sleeps away a large portion of his shift and leaves the kitchen a total disaster before clocking out.

I just got here so it's not right for me to start firing people, especially since we don't have anyone to replace him anyways. I must give people the chance to prove themselves, the same way I must prove myself. Yet, I can't help but wonder how long the new dietary manager will last and what type of impact he will have on the already horrible dining experience. He was hired after Adult Protective Services came in regarding the slop complaint so that wasn't on his watch. But now, several weeks into his position, the food isn't much better, and the portion sizes are still a joke for 300lb grown folks. The residents said they either didn't receive meals, or meals would often be hours late, cold, and portioned for toddlers. All of this has been substantiated by me within my first days of working at Heaven Forbid Senior Living. The food is a joke. But how can the residents afford to order so much take out?

Two weeks in

I just got access to the first payroll. 400+ hours of overtime! WTF? And this has been consistent for how long? When I interviewed for this position, I was told, "we're fully staffed with tenured employees." It sounded too good to be true, and it most certainly was. I was told we are deficiency free, then learned Adult Protective Services recently came in on a complaint that residents were being served slop if they were being served any food at all. Yet, the department of licensing only found minor citations. In the two weeks I have been here I have been knee-deep in fall investigations one of which no one knows anything about but there's an elderly woman with dementia who sustained a broken bone in the memory care unit. Oh yeah, and we have an employee dedicated to fall investigations because they happen all throughout the day, every single day.

I've already had to speak with a resident about not sexually harassing the female staff since I now have several written complaints. Allegedly he likes vodka and gets belligerent when drinking. Another resident is allegedly on crystal-meth, carries a knife and gets physically confrontational but supposedly hasn't done so in a while. There is so much to do, and each day I clear off my desk still with much to do. Thankfully we have made some progress; all residents are being fed 3 meals a day now, and we found some plates so our residents in memory care are being served hot food on plates via the new heated food transport cart I bought with expedited delivery. Since it's not in the budget I most likely won't be reimbursed for the $1,000.00 piece of equipment. But it's demoralizing seeing confused elders at the end of their lives being served out of Styrofoam boxes when it's not necessary.

It's not even 9 o'clock in the morning and I already got a phone call from the Medicaid case manager regarding a resident's daughter screaming in her ear. The case manager and I speak often regarding the residents she manages so we're both aware of the specific families that fly off the rails. The case manager said the daughter was screaming at her, not talking loudly but SCREAMING in her ear about food and how her mom didn't get any dinner when she got back from the hospital last night and no one answered the phone when she called and called and on and on.

The case manager called to give me a heads-up, then I prepared myself and rang the resident's daughter. I made sure to tell her I had witnesses listening on speaker phone conference, and yes, she was screaming at all of us, too. But this is a simple problem to fix. I wish all problems were this simple. We now place extra meals in the reach-in refrigerator after dinner service in case someone returns late or gets hungry in the middle of the night. A peanut butter and jelly sandwich is not dinner but if someone wants something light, we also have that and a few other options available. Unfortunately, the really long list of problematic concerns, each which is very fixable with a little direction and team workers, continues to plague us when workers who revert to, "but we've always done it that way." Well, 'that way' is old and outdated.

The new 'always available extra meals in the refrigerator' service is due to repeated complaints from residents and families. I was texting back and forth with a different upset family member until after 10:00 PM the other night because her mom didn't get any dinner after coming back from an appointment. She went on and on but at least that was an easy fix. It's not ideal for families to have the executive director's cell phone number, but how else are the residents going to be heard when there is no one to answer the front desk phones after I leave. Yes, a boundary has been crossed. Now that I am here, for the first time in many years management is in the building past the hour of 3:00 PM. But I'm not staying past 7 on a regular basis. And I answer my phone. But apparently after I leave there is no one to answer the phone at the front desk. I just learned the phones are supposed to roll over to a manager on duty. The problem is the MOD never answers when the phone rings. What a mess! Please, if you happen to be on-call, keep your ringer turned on and answer the phone when it rings.

Why is it so hard for caregivers to carry and answer the phone at night? "Pharmacy is at the door with a STAT delivery! Please answer the door. Please answer the phone so you'll hear the delivery guy calling, and when families call." Not even the overnight med-tech is willing to answer the phones I was told, "No. He has a bad attitude and we're just lucky to have him because he's the only med-tech at night. We're lucky to have him, a caregiver in assisted living, and a caregiver in memory care." One floating med-tech and two caregivers for 70-80 high acuity heavy wetting residents. At least there aren't a lot of medications to be given at night, mostly PRN (as needed) if any. So, he can help the caregivers on the floor. Oh no! He doesn't do diaper changes. And in reviewing the cameras it's evident the caregivers don't either.

Now I've just learned managers have been using the company card for restaurant food delivery multiple times a week and this has been either permissible or overlooked for years. They average spending over $1,000 per month on takeout food and coffee, but the budget doesn't allow for improving the quality of food for the residents. Something is amiss. I'm still two weeks in and this place is already wearing on me. But at least my nurse just started, and we have plates to reopen the dining room. Now to get dining room chairs and train the servers to alleviate the cold food complaints and get rid of the excessive to-go trash.

Today we began implementing fresh iced water, hot coffee, and snacks in the bistro. We also have a popcorn cart, so starting tomorrow a server will make popcorn daily at 2:00 PM for the residents and their guests. And my sister donated a nice side by side refrigerator for bistro snacks. Little things like that help subdue complaints about other minor issues.

Three weeks in

Our new nurse started over five days ago and there are already red flags. She appears to take a lot of smoke breaks and not nearly enough notes because she keeps asking the same questions and must be retrained on way too many basic things. Now, here we go with the nurse! How long will this brand-new nurse last? If there's one thing I have learned, it's that even many years of experience doesn't necessarily make someone right for a director's position. The chef has over 15 years of experience and is failing because his ego is an anchor. The nurse has over 30 years of experience yet struggles to put the cigarette down for long enough to stop complaining about how hard the job is. I know this place is challenging and I told you during the interview process that I need help! I need strong leaders with backbones that will work harder than ever before to get this busted ship off the reef and hold people accountable to rowing this bad boy. I can't have a nurse that needs floaties, and I can't have leadership outside talking mess while smoking with the residents and caregivers. I will have another talk with her because I need help. At least this nurse has received multiple days of training. Most nurses in assisted livings are thrown in. Most employees in general are thrown in to sink or swim, but she has been trained.

I spoke with her again, coaching and trying to be supportive, but today she broke down crying. "It's just too much for one nurse! And last weekend I didn't know what to do and the regional nurse wasn't helping me!" Last Saturday was my anniversary, so I was several hours away in a cabin when the call came in from my new nurse who was really upset. "A resident is on the ledge and threatening to jump!" I told her everything was going to be fine and to hang up and call 911. I took a moment to process - we have a suicidal resident that just made an attempt, so he needs behavioral health services. I called her back and she sounded overwhelmed, so my husband and I packed up and started driving to the community. Three hours later I arrived, surprisingly without a speeding ticket, and learned they convinced the resident to come back inside the building. I asked the nurse if 911 arrived and she said they didn't take her seriously and told her to call the crisis hotline who would come out to assess the situation. And I thought to myself, "by that time he could have been a splattered corpse on the ground." I picked up the phone, dialed 911, and told the dispatcher, "We have a resident that just attempted suicide by jumping off our building, I need someone here now!" It may have been a whole two or three minutes later when the fire department pulled into the parking lot with sirens blaring. Then the ambulance arrived and took him to the hospital for evaluation before admitting him to a geriatric-psyche hospital.

Our current marketing director was three months in and almost out the door when I started. Disappointed, she was the only leader that worked a full 8-hour day until I got here. She was also upset that there hasn't been a nurse to follow through on the care services she has been promising to new move ins. "I feel like a liar." That's what the marketer told me, and I can't blame her. I've been in her shoes many times. No telling how long before she gives notice and I presume her resume has already been updated, just like everyone else's.

Before I came aboard the marketer was receiving all the staff, family, and resident complaints, so she was in operations way too deep to focus on sales. Every day has brought some new 'B.S.' the marketer feels compelled to listen to since she has an HR background and she wants everyone to be at least a little happy in this place. Time will tell in no time at all. Still, she is doing well enough because she's had ten move ins in the past month or so. The pressure is on because the census is low. Even at 80 residents, that still leaves 70 more to move in and heaven forbid any residents move out or die. Before I arrived, the marketer had to be talked off the edge of quitting because of the lack of leadership. I can tell she will probably give her two weeks' notice soon. Man, I'm trying, and I see she and a couple of other people are trying too, but it sure feels like I'm alone in this battle.

The activity director finally spoke to me on my 4th day out of absolute necessity after I demanded she and I speak. She usually tries to avoid me, but we need to interact, you know, for the service of our residents. "I just ain't feeling it, I'm burnt out," were her first introductory words to me when I asked how I could support her department. Yeah, that was my fourth day on the job. I am trying to be super patient because I realize my track record has been to fire the activity director, of whichever community I manage, within my first few weeks of working because the activity programs usually stink. It's not ok for activity directors to have piss-poor attitudes and be unwilling to improve on the programming. We all have room for improvement. I come in smiling and bubbling every day, and that's what is needed from activity directors. We need activity directors that get residents hyped up and ready to have some fun. Not a burnt-out Eeyore. I am an imperfect human that can't wait until the activity director's bad attitude toting self falls off this ship because she needs to go! How are you even going to remain working here if you won't speak with your supervisor? The activity calendar is boring, the bulletin board looks childish, snack time is not an activity for residents that still drive even if they do happen to live in assisted living, and she's barely even here because she's always taking time off. I have tried to be patient, but the residents are bored, and her attitude is poor.

The business office manager is a nice young woman that has been fit into every peg of every department at one time or another over the past five years. Yet, she isn't into keeping up with state compliance so why is she in the business office? Oh, because no one wants the job. Why hasn't anyone checked to make sure she was keeping records in compliance? Because corporate doesn't care. She appears to be indifferent to the issues in this facility and likely also wondering how long I will be there. But she does see that I care and I'm working my tail off to improve the living conditions. She acts like she's on board, but she too has been accountable to no one, and has been used to strolling in and out at whatever time. Before I arrived, she and Pretender spent a lot of time together sitting around gossiping and shooting the breeze with another two sloths, all of whom would tell you today that, "they're here for the residents". There's no urgency with her, or with anyone at Heaven Forbid for that matter. The rats have been running the show for decades and running good managers and employees away when they attempt to make a difference. They haven't been held accountable by anyone and they simply turn their eyes to the abuse and neglect, pay period after pay period. The coldest hearts thus far.

Now my new nurse is crying to the dietary manager about the marketer director not liking her because she doesn't know what to do with new admission doctor's orders. "It has nothing to do with the marketer liking you or not. She has a job to do. We did this training with you last week, and we went over it again yesterday as a group." This nurse is making me question my own sanity. "Again, check through the doctor's order, the history and physical (H&P), and look over the list of medications. If the prospective resident is on any antipsychotics, then we need more information regarding potential behaviors." 30 years of experience and she hasn't ever seen or read a doctor's order? It hurts my heart that with this terrible nursing shortage, I already feel the need to find a new nurse, again. The 30-year veteran nurse lasted around one month before I had to let her go. The caregivers can't see you crying, and you shouldn't be outside smoking with the residents and complaining about how hard your job is to them. I feel like my leadership team is dragging in one way or another and only my marketing department really wants to make it work.

2 Months in

I need to get away for a few days. Even the president of the United States takes time off to decompress all the while being kept abreast of any serious situations that arise while away. A call came in that only one caregiver showed up to work. There was a misunderstanding with the schedule or people are being spiteful or something because only one caregiver showed up to work today. I am 3000 miles away trying to gain some peace of mind and there's only one caregiver to care for 90 residents who are severe fall risks, and many of whom have dementia, are incontinent, and bed bound. My office manager called caregivers and offered them $200 cash bonuses to come in so two people are coming in.

Then I got a call from the regional marketing director who got a call about no staff inside the sister community. She was asking if we could spare any caregivers. She said, "Our sister community is in desperation since their nurse just quit after no caregivers showed up to work. The nurse said she's tired of filling shifts and she walked out. Their executive director is out of town, so they have no one to take care of the residents. He has been calling staffing agencies to see if they can get someone here right away to cover the open shifts, but the staffing agencies said they don't have any caregivers available either." She continued, "Me and the business office manager are heading over there now to keep the residents safe."

Now we have to offer caregivers $200 bonuses to come to work on top of their already increased hourly rate just to have warm bodies in the community scrolling through their phones. And no one showed up to work at our sister community, at all, and the nurse walked out.

Dragging my way to three months in.

Another Monday with High Hopes although I can't say that I really have much pep in my step knowing something crazy likely awaits my arrival. It's not a good neighborhood but it is what it is and assisted livings need to accommodate people of every background and income level. Each morning as I approach Heaven Forbid Senior Living, I drive around the perimeter of the building to chase away homeless people sleeping in various corners and next to the dumpsters, and out front by the sign, sitting in the grass with their tents spread and soiled articles of cloth strung here, there, and everywhere. One lady is a frequent offender showering on the side of the building next to the street, indecent exposure? She bares it all. But it's not safe for a woman to shower outside at night so she does it in broad daylight. To dodge me she showers at various times of the day knowing I cannot be outside to run her away all the time.

Made it to three months in but it feels like 9 months of hard labor.

It's my third month as the executive director and thank goodness there are no homeless people by this dumpster this morning. I'm rounding the corner now and, thankfully there's no homeless people sitting there either. Those two locations are the most frequently inhabited.

My boss was here today, and I voiced my concerns about the many challenges I'm facing. He could clearly feel my frustration and said, "just hang in there with us and this time next year your salary will double." I am already making $100K per year. And he's telling me to look away and I will make twice as much next year. What the heck am I doing here?

A new resident who recently moved into memory care fell and the fall was unwitnessed. The resident had a skin tear on the face which to me indicates a head injury. When in doubt send them out! That is the motto one of my favorite nurses from years ago instilled in my head, and what I have been training on week after week and month after month. Unfortunately, it's almost impossible to get these tenured employees to do the right thing since they were taught over the years not to call 911 due to having pretend nurses as bosses. An incident was written but supposedly the report was not given to the oncoming shift, nor was information about the fall relayed.

Someone put her back in bed and hours went by. The morning shift got the resident to the dining room, and she complained of pain, so a medication assistant gave a pain med. Then, the resident face-planted into her food...and neither caregivers nor medication assistants questioned that there is something wrong. Training after training on resident falls and when in doubt send them out! But no. Instead, they put her to bed, again, all the while knowing something wasn't right about this resident. More hours go by, more complaints of pain and more pain medications. Now, it's nighttime and one of the family members comes to visit realizing there was indeed something wrong. Thankfully the family demanded their beloved be sent to the emergency room. Yet, this is probably 14 or more hours after the actual fall.

The emergency room revealed a broken bone and of course the family was rightfully vexed. They had just moved their loved one in a few weeks ago and now this. I have not quite made it to my four-month anniversary since it is three days away. But I sure do question why I am still the executive director in a location where my hands are tied, where we don't have enough caregivers to care for the residents we already have, where corporate is upset because I just denied around a half dozen move-in's due to not having a nurse and the lack of care so we haven't had a move in in almost a month. And now that resident is in the hospital.

Incoming email from my regional marketing director to me and several other executive leaders.

Hello

The uptick in leads has increased significantly. As you know we have moved 8 new residents and are working on a number of leads for next month. I am concerned about the clinical department with nursing (or lack of) and caregiving/MedTech staffing in this community, and we will need to address this from the marketing standpoint in the coming months. We are also working closely with the maintenance team to open empty rooms as quickly as possible so we can accommodate the move-ins. I have helped with the new discovery room, the front lobby area, and the resident dining room to create pleasing aesthetics for residents, tours, and events.

I have done some outreach however we will need to develop this more as the rehabs and hospitals begin to reopen.

We have lost the following leads in the past month due to a number of issues:

1. *Mr. XXXX - 2 person transfer and stage 1 wound STAFFING*

2. *Ms. XXXX - hourly checks to turn, incontinent, redness on buttocks STAFFING*

3. *Mr. XXXXX - g-tube and night checks STAFFING*

4. *Mrs. XXXXX - high acuity STAFFING*

My take on these losses is that clearing up staffing issues and getting a nurse on board will alleviate some of the rejections. XXXX is working on 3-4 new leads that should come through soon, we are waiting on rehab to be completed.

Presently we are awaiting a full-time nurse in the community and my suggestion would be that due to the number of changes the staff is experiencing, a full-time nurse can provide consistency, reliability, less confusion, cohesion, and trust.

*- **XXXX, Regional Director of Sales and Marketing***

I have been here for almost four months, but I don't think I'll survive to nine. It's Monday morning and a subpoena for medical records awaited me as I walked through the door. Apparently, the resident died. She moved in a few weeks ago and now she's dead because the caregivers put her back to bed after she had an unwitnessed fall in the bathroom and broke her neck. She is being autopsied and a full investigation is underway. Monday, a subpoena, and finally another new nurse started. And a cook just walked off the job. So, what's going on in the kitchen now?

Someone accused someone else of racism and it became a screaming match. Since I wasn't there, I've only gotten reports from witnesses and of course the peanut gallery that heard stories from someone else, so they think they really know what happened. Let's check in on our new nurse, how is your first day of training? My nurses' sentiments, "It's a black hole, and the further I reach in the more crap I pull out."

It's Tuesday morning, two days until my four-month anniversary. What will today bring? I just got off a conference call regarding Covid compliance and documenting. Apparently, a week or so ago Department of Health Services went into our sister community to conduct the annual survey. Again, minor deficiencies found but one citation was due to that location not having a Covid protocol. Thankfully, I have that in place in the community I am managing. Interesting enough, our sister community just rehired the nurse that walked off the job a few weeks ago when no staff showed up. She literally abandoned her job and now she just got rehired because there aren't any nurses applying.

Tuesday also brought a resident that called hospice because she wanted to commit suicide and thought they would help her do it. Then came a bag full of crystal meth from out of a resident's room. I called the police and had them confiscate it and make a report. Crystal Meth is illegal, and we manage his medications anyways so I will be giving him a formal eviction notice after the paperwork from the police department is completed. And that means he may end up homeless like he was once before.

The first addict in the building I didn't get a chance to kick out because he left one night and never returned. He left all his personal belongings and vanished back to the streets wheelchair bound with serious medical illnesses...a few days fresh from getting out of the hospital. His drug of choice was heroine and if he's not dead then he's probably on the streets now. I learned his Medicaid case manager may not assist him with rehabilitation which he likely isn't interested in anyways. I mean he's been doing drugs for decades so it would be hard convincing him to quit now. It's a new day so of course there are new issues to battle. One resident just came to my office freaking out about an arrest warrant he just received in the mail because he thought he could get away with something. "I'm sorry. I don't know what to tell you!"

Adult protective services called regarding a complaint of abuse and neglect on a resident who had severe breathing problems and passed away two weeks ago. I got a call from a recruiter headhunting for another executive director position in a troubled assisted living and memory care community. I'm at the point now where I wonder are there any assisted livings out there that don't have serious problems? Even the nicest places have issues, but this place is over the top negligent and careless and I am so tired of talking to adult protective services, state surveyors, ombudsman, the crisis teams, and police officers. It's getting to me.

Today makes my four-month anniversary, 7:15 AM on this Monday morning. My new nurse is not unfamiliar to the tenured staff members some of whom have already expressed their disdain for her. One has even accused this new nurse of stealing narcotics. So now we must wonder if the person making the allegation is simply hateful and potentially a ringleader that works up other staff members. Again, time will tell and no time at all.

Four and a half months: My integrity is compromised, and I'm tapping out.

On the very last day of my employment as the executive director of Heaven Forbid, the headline news read the following about an assisted living in Mesa, Arizona, "90-year-old found dead in sweltering vehicle". Placed in a memory care community, the United States veteran was never removed from the vehicle after returning from a morning appointment. He was left in the sweltering transport van in the middle of the desert summer heat, windows closed all afternoon, all night, all next morning, until his wife of 67 years came to visit, and no one knew where he was.

No one noticed when he wasn't at dinner. The overnight shift didn't notice he wasn't in his bed when doing nightly checks and brief changes. No one asked where he was the next day at breakfast. And no one noticed missed medication passes and medication errors for the previous night or that morning's med pass. No one noticed? But they signed off indicating they gave him night medications. Do they even do daily and nightly checks and brief changes? I can't imagine the agony he must've felt confined in the back of the 153°F transport van. I can't fathom the grief of everyone involved in yesterday's news. My throat swelled and tears welled in my eyes for that poor man, for his suffering, for his life to end that way, for his wife's pain, for the constant pain she will have to live with, for their family. It's horrific! What's not news is that many workers don't bother to notice when a resident isn't there for breakfast, lunch, dinner, med passes and other scheduled care services that cost thousands of dollars. And no one asks questions, just assumes they're with family.

That could have happened at Heaven Forbid! It could've happened at a few other 'half-ass' communities I've worked in and know of due to sub-par care by people on their devices or simply looking the other way. The executive director's hands are tied because they can't find enough good caregivers to work anymore than I can. The job fair I hosted on my last day (literally yesterday) as my final attempt to set up the troubled community for success, that last effort job fair resulted in not one applicant coming in. Not even 1. Maybe it was the rain that kept good applicants away. Or maybe it's the same reasons there haven't been many applicants in the past 4 months of my managing the community…it's very hard work for just above minimum wage and the government pays people to stay home right now anyways. Even before the pandemic it was a struggle to find good people willing to do the hard work for little pay. How can executive directors and facility managers get rid of the bad attitudes and complacent employees if we can't replace them with good ones. Why aren't people showing up to interviews? We need lots of employees to care for multitudes of residents and there are three 8-hour shifts to cover.

The Morning After

As I type this morning, it's 9:18 AM and I realize I am still on the community's cell phone group-chat-line because my incoming text literally reads, word for word, "What time is memory care getting breakfast?" WHAT? It's almost 9:30 in the morning! Breakfast is at the very same time every single day, 7:00 AM! Why haven't the most vulnerable residents, the dementia population who needs structure, received breakfast yet? Lunch is supposed to start in two hours. After all these months of guiding and coaching to ensure residents receive quality food, on time, every day, after all the trainings and bits of progress here and there, and it's already falling apart. It hasn't even been 24 hours since I left.

Yesterday's heart wrenching headline of that poor 90-year-old man could have easily happened at Heaven Forbid. I couldn't even go out of town without distressing phone calls so my choice to leave was necessary to maintain my own sanity. Yet, it's undoubtedly disturbing to think of what may happen to the residents I left behind. They have no choice but to remain there just like the residents in the other communities with fatally flawed care.

CHAPTER SEVEN

'Conjugal' Visits

After pouring myself into Heaven Forbid Senior Living, I realized it wasn't worth sacrificing my sanity, health, and personal life. I walked away yet the residents had no choice but to stay. I'm now managing a much nicer assisted living community mainly for people with dementia, but it's far from perfect as with any business run by the imperfect likes of me. The common denominator with each location is days of both sunshine and stormy weather.

There are vacant rooms that need to be filled and people who will soon pass away, so I need a pipeline of new hot leads that will convert into move-ins right away. Now offering ½ off the one-time non-refundable community fee. Here's hoping for a Hospice or Home Health referral over the referral agency leads we must pay thousands of dollars for. Hospice refers to us and we refer to them.

It has only been a few weeks in my new executive director position and it's like déjà vu. This is a nice facility, but all locations have issues especially with employees and families that behave badly. So here are a few more recordings before ending the book to show what it's like inside of a nice, assisted living … remembering not all locations are pitiful like Heaven Forbid Senior Living.

Sunday

———◆———

I just got a call-off for the overnight shift, so I am on my way in to cover since no other caregivers can go in. I am enroute to work and just received another phone call, a different caregiver is calling off for tomorrow morning. That means although I have been working operations all day, I must work from 10PM tonight, overnight, until tomorrow at 2 o'clock in the afternoon with hopes that my 2 PM person will show up because by then I will be about falling over.

I have now been sent multiple pictures of employees sleeping on the job overnight when they should be ensuring residents are not in urine-soaked briefs. Before I got here a resident was found with a bloody head and no one knew she had fallen until morning shift discovered it.

Tuesday

———◆———

I woke up this morning at 2:30 AM and decided to check the cameras. Sure enough, caregivers were sleeping on the job in the recliner chairs in the living room so I called the community. I watched the med tech awaken and walk across the room towards the office to answer the phone. "How are things going?" I asked. The MedTech replied, "What are you doing up this late?" I replied everything that happens in the community is my responsibility so I'm calling to make sure all the residents are dry and being tended to and that caregivers are not sleeping on the job.

The MedTech replied, "things are going well and almost everything is done". I then told her to wake up the other caregiver and make sure no one is sleeping while they are on the clock. We hung up the phone, and I watched her on the camera wake the other caregiver who began throwing her arms in the air ranting, vexed about having to wake up and work. This is not a Medicaid subsidized building, and this is not a group-home. All the residents are privately paying over $6,000 per month and not for caregivers to sleep. Four hours later, I received a call from the vexed caregiver calling off for tonight. Hopefully by the end of this week I will have her shifts filled by a new employee that understands the importance of remaining awake to do what's in the best interests of the residents.

Wednesday

I got a text message from a caregiver with a picture attached just after 6 o'clock in the morning. The picture was of a resident naked from the waist down laying on a blue mat on the floor beside her bed and there were feces everywhere. I was told night-shift caregivers said they did rounds at 5:00 AM signing off indicating everyone's briefs had been changed. Yet the feces on her were dry. There's no telling how long she laid on that floor, cold and covered in her own excrement. A lot of changes will be made in this facility, and I will recreate the image for the cover of this book.

3 months in - Thursday

———◆———

Tomorrow is my birthday and I have gotten call offs for second shift today, and overnight tonight. Thankfully I was able to cover the call off for tonight so I can go home around 10 PM and get some sleep.

Friday

———◆———

Happy birthday to me came with another call off for second shift today, tomorrow, Sunday and Monday. It also came with positive COVID-19 test results. Four of our residents just tested positive and several more have symptoms yet tested negative. Face it, we're in each other's faces. Employees and visitors that unknowingly spit when they speak and refuse to wear a mask are fighting against infection control best practices. The dementia residents aren't going out to catch it at stores and stations, so someone must have brought it in. Now I must lock down the entire facility. Thankfully the virus has mutated at least a half a dozen times over the past few years of the pandemic and it may not be quite as deadly, or whatever the new findings say, so fingers crossed.

I sent an email to all families alerting them to the positive COVID cases and the need for lockdown. Almost everyone was understanding except for one challenging family member who replied. "Do you have a caregiver dedicated to every resident positive for COVID?" As if assisted-living facilities can provide one on one care. We barely have enough caregivers as it is because people don't show up to interviews and first days on the job on top of the non-stop time off requests.

I'm the executive director and I'm filling in for a call-off caregiver on my birthday. Oh, how I wish for the very best committed caregivers to be here now tending to your mom's every whim. I probably want that more than you do at this moment because I should be working a cocktail right now. But that's just a dream. I let the family know that it is impossible for an assisted living to provide one on one care for every resident especially when people don't want to work. Even caregiver registry companies struggle to find people who want to work.

From before the day I started, this family feels the assisted living facility can't do anything right. Their mother has multiple medical problems. advanced cognitive impairments, and she frequently roams in and out of other's rooms which is to be expected with her condition. I met the family member at the door to ensure she received my email regarding positive cases of COVID-19 in the building and that visitation is restricted effective today. She said, "This is a really inconvenient time for me." I agreed and replied, "Yes, for me too because it's my birthday."

The openly agitated daughter had a tube of diaper rash ointment that she accuses our staff of misplacing. She said, "this is the fourth tube of cream I have brought in the past few weeks and your staff keeps losing it or throwing it away." I reminded her that this is an assisted living facility that has turned into a Dementia care facility and residents, including her mother, constantly wander in and out of other people's rooms. I went on to say that corporate has already been notified that locked medicine cabinets should be installed in every resident bathroom for safety precautions. But that wasn't good enough. Then she attempted to hand me some hard chocolaty edible thing in a small Tupperware container to give her mother which I refused because we don't have a doctor's order for whatever that is. "You can give her whatever you want to, but we are under strict guidelines and rules." That just upset her more.

Passive-aggressively threatening to move her mom to a different place, she said she and her sisters will have a meeting to determine next steps in their mom's care ... and I reacted with relief words of, "Yes! You should have that meeting right away." We may need high census. But we don't have to tolerate families that make employees cringe when they enter the building. I wheeled her mom outside and the chocolaty Tupperware surprise was consumed. Now her mom has tested positive for the virus, too.

It is still my birthday weekend. Since it's a holiday I anticipated call offs. I worked until very late on my birthday last night covering a call off, and now I'm here again on a Saturday covering another call off. I left work six hours ago, got home, and now just received two call offs for the morning shift. So, I must take a nap and head back to work, again. I can't leave only one or two caregivers to take care of multiples of residents. My over-the-hill birthday weekend brings me face to face with the dreaded thought of living life to a ripe old age in our country knowing what I know.

4 months in

I am on my way to work, and I just got a distressing message from a caregiver at Heaven Forbid Senior Living. I no longer work there and thank goodness for that because it was an absolute $#!+ Show! Over a year later caregivers still call me crying about how horrible things have gotten and what to do about helping resident ABC. "It was bad before I got there, worse than anyone would have anticipated, and I couldn't take it more than five months because I couldn't stand seeing the resident's pain. There's nothing I can do. I'm not employed there anymore." The caregiver vented on the phone for almost an hour before I stopped her instructing, "Call the state!". She ended by saying there are bedbugs in almost every single room now and you can see them crawling on the couch and chairs in the common areas.

There were bugs before I got there, and the state and Adult Protective Services called me several times about it. But by the time I left we visibly narrowed it down to only one room because pest control damn-near lived in the building. It was the room of a hoarder that treasured every object and greeting card she'd ever acquired. Her room was packed. Extermination invoices were outrageously expensive but at least there weren't bugs and rats visibly crawling around in the daytime or jumping out at staff members. I knew they'd never really go away since that facility was colonized by critters many, many generations ago. They are still lively at night. And so are the residents and employees taking smoke breaks and shots of vodka, blazing dab-pens, and doing whatever else they do in the gazebo. Heaven Forbid, that place is a trip.

My experience from the first facility I worked in, Whispering Winds, comes in handy as infestations were deeply rooted into the foundation of that place, too. Both locations are subsidized by Medicaid. Whispering Winds still looks the same as it did back then. It still has the very same granite-top desk the fed-up office manager's husband never got paid for. That facility was initially owned by one of the companies highlighted in the PBS documentary, then it was sold to another shady company, then it got sold again, acquisition after acquisition, management company after management company. Worst case scenario assisted livings are added to another senior living company's portfolio only to be dumped along to another company.

Fast forward 15 years into my senior living career and Whispering Winds isn't too much better than Heaven-Forbid Senior Living – which is one of the worst I have known. The dysfunction in location after location is no secret to visitors and industry partners. Medicaid case managers, local referral agents, hospices, home health companies, and many others are in and out of the facilities all the time. Prospect residents referred to and living in the broken facilities are or were broke themselves, destitute, and/or desperate. Workers inside are disengaged if they show up at all, and the potential for work compensation claims, lawsuits and state citations weighs heavily on the executive director's minds.

99

"Didn't you hear it on the news, during COVID, a resident went to the courtyard and one of the landscapers left the door propped open. The resident wandered away and no one could find him. He was eventually found in an empty warehouse dead from the sweltering heat. That same facility was in the news again; a

resident punched and killed another resident. Every employee had COVID, every resident had COVID, and there you have that. There's always a worry of - will they follow your protocols?"

A new lead just came in from a referral agent for a severely depressed resident who is a bedbound, two-person transfer-Hoyer lift with advanced vascular dementia. The resident has right-side paralysis from a stroke, a foley catheter, has been known to be combative, and requires total care. Knowing much of the staff is unreliable and we're always hiring new caregivers, how comfortable would you feel being accountable to the family of this resident, and being the same for others with similar medical conditions?

Is this beyond assisted living's scope of practice? I am now working with a lead that has an ostomy and a feeding tube because she is suicidal by trying to starve herself. "I just want to die!" That's what the retired nurse kept saying but her relatives wanted differently. We have empty beds so she's our new admission. She came to us weighing around 70 pounds and her relatives were adamant that she participates in physical therapy, but she was weak and refused. Having been wasting away in a hospital bed for however many months made her legs weak as twigs so there wasn't going to be any bearing of weight anyways. She can barely breathe because she lacks strength in her chest muscles, and she can barely keep her eyes open. We had to put her medications into the feeding tube along with the liquid-protein supplement drink. Death with Dignity is not yet legal in the state of Arizona, even though there is a massive retirement population, so we did our best to get nourishment in her. The poor lady was miserable, depressed and in pain. We finally convinced the family and got her on Hospice a few days later. She passed within ten days of admission.

That poses a very personal question for each of us. If you are physically and/or mentally falling apart, drooling, incontinent, immobile, staring into space and detached from reality, completely dependent on others for care, would you want to live in an assisted living or dementia care facility? Can you and are you willing to pay five to ten or more thousand dollars per month for potentially sub-par care provided by cold-hearted warm-bodies that really don't care? Is it dignified to keep pushing pills, tubes, and surgeries to keep people alive even if they're quality of life is poor?

When the comedian actor Robin Williams took his own life after being diagnosed with a terminal illness that would rob him of his personality, memory, and ability to remain in control of his life, it made me ponder the question of my own destiny knowing dementia is expected to increase. I still eat many items of the standard American diet which science has proven to cause the diseases that lead to dementia. It's a question we should all answer, in writing, in our living will and final wishes. What do they say? Everyone is an accident or illness away from being completely dependent on others every day. The residents keep saying, "Where did the time go? I don't feel like I'm 90 years old, I still feel like I'm 50." You don't have to be old to need help. And with all the heart-disease plaguing out country, needing help isn't too far off into the future.

100

"I've been told by corporate to stop calling it high acuity because we don't work in a hospital. But I call it what it is, we are admitting high-acuity resident. Don't sugar coat and change the terms because it gives a false impression of the care you provide."

Last week I admitted an 80-year-old lady who was living in her own home taking care of her ailing husband. A month prior she was still gardening, cooking, driving, and shopping, until she got into a terrible car accident. Her injuries, although bad, didn't take her life. It was the stage-4 pressure ulcers she developed after being discharged from the hospital into an understaffed rehabilitation facility that took her out.

When she arrived in my facility her adult children thought she'd become well enough for physical therapy. They didn't understand the Hospice evaluation we ordered was for end-of-life comfort care. Her decline happened quickly so the hard-conversation and education on her prognosis caught the family by surprise. "It's time to prepare for her death. Which funeral home do you prefer?" It was devastating to see the emotional pain on her son's face. "But she was just fine last month. We should have brought her here sooner." Indeed, she qualified for Hospice and was prescribed liquid morphine for pain management. Her children were against the morphine thinking she may become addicted to narcotics, so my nurse had to educate the family that addiction is the last thing to worry about. "She's in pain and she's dying."

Last month the spunky silver-haired lady was caring for her spouse and handling her business. She was on Hospice services for less than 72 hours before she passed away in our facility. It was around 7 o'clock in the morning when the gurney was wheeled though the hallway and out the door, draped with a white sheet covering her remains. Her relatives stared out of the window with tears streaming down their cheeks in disbelief as they watched her being loaded into the back of the transport van. Once the van drove off, the family tearfully hauled the furniture they brought in only a few days prior out of the building. If only the rehab facilities had enough CNAs and Nurses working maybe she would have been turned more often to prevent pressure ulcers from developing.

For the less-than three days she lived in the facility, and we still had to pay over $1500 in fees to the referral company on top of employee salaries, mortgage, electricity, food, and other business expenses. Talk about losing money on admissions. Well, at least the family was so grateful that they donated the remaining month's fees so this time we weren't out of pocket but families donating money is not the norm.

Too often families are not reasonable, and they bring in every pill they can find to make mom better. Or possibly worse, they talk the physicians and neurologists out of prescribing anxiety and pain management medications out of fear of addiction. One of my residents has 14 doctors. I can't help but wonder if she's being used as a pin cushion and now contemplate getting Adult Protective Services involved. I got a fax just yesterday from a physician saying, "we didn't prescribe that." The spouse will just go to another doctor if they don't like what their first one said. Or the second one. Or the third one. Some families are beyond challenging.

101

——◆——

"One lady has to take so many pills. Before breakfast she has to take almost a dozen pills on an empty stomach, so she gets nauseous. The other day she threw-up her pills like ten minutes later. At 8:00 AM she has to take more pills with her breakfast. Then before noon she has to take more pills. And it's like that all day long until her last scheduled medications at 10:00 PM. The med cart is filled with her bottles of pills and it's like every day a doctor discontinues a medication and starts her on a new one. The

husband brings in bottle after bottle of medications and there are a bunch of different doctors prescribing her meds. I bet each doctor doesn't even know what the other doctors are prescribing, or that the other doctors even exist."

102

—◆—

"A daughter and her husband thought they were advocates for the world. They convinced hospice to keep upping the morphine when my resident didn't need it. And then finally her mom passed away. The daughter came in and said our caregiver was giving her the wrong dose because someone put the thought of litigation in her mind. We had a meeting with the family and her husband said, "we're going to own this thing. And she starts crying uncontrollably, "oh my mom" then it was you were taunting my mother. I went into her room, it was right before easter weekend and she said, "there's' nothing but bunnies. Fk'ing bunnies. You did this intentionally!" And she ran into the bathroom and we were like this is whackadoodle. And then the husband said, "I manage a tire shop. I know business and were going to own this business if you don't do something for us." I said you know I'm just a manager in a huge corporation, I can't just write you a check. Come to find out they lost their home or whatever and they were looking for a payout and we refunded the last month, and they just went away. And I'm on the hotline and on the phone with corporate about possible litigation about Fk'ing Bunnies! She had a picture of her mom, and she was rocking. It looked so staged."

103

———◆———

"*Every afternoon a husband would drive to the facility to visit his wife in the memory care unit just to have sex with her. The resident was really confused with dementia, and she didn't recognize him, so she thought she was being raped. She was far advanced in her dementia and she couldn't scream anymore but the caregivers said they could hear her fighting and whimpering. When he was done, he would just leave her there naked, shaking, and laying in filth for our caregivers to calm her down and clean her up. I didn't know what to do so I called the state and they said there's nothing I could do because that's her husband and he's her power of attorney. So, I called my boss and again I was told there's nothing we can do but it breaks my heart for her to keep going through that.*"

My nurse texted me, "Resident XYZ will likely pass away today or tomorrow. I already contacted the family and have the human release forms ready." I feel for the family, and now have another room that needs to be filled ASAP. I feel heartless thinking more about filling the room than sending condolence flowers. No lost revenue days tinnitus keeps me dizzy.

Then I got a text from this weekend's ghost caregiver. She is behaving like the other caregivers we must rely on to care for, and frequently turn, high acuity residents that really should have 24-hour nursing services. She, along with others, is not reliable. I took a screen shot of her text and sent to my nurse. The text literally reads, "Hi I apologize for not been able to respond but I have not been feeling well." Second text, "sore throat and cough." I don't have the patience to reply yet. I feel like saying, "Come on! We've been calling and texting trying to get ahold of you for days and you just now reply after not showing up."

I can't come in because I have a headache – So take some over-the-counter meds and get to work. I can't come in because my car won't start - I will give you a ride or since you only live a few blocks away put one foot in front of the other and start walking like people did for hundreds if not thousands of years. I can't come in because I have a sore throat and cough – So take some meds and put on a mask. We were working while we were sick with COVID-19. Does your sore throat really have you out of commission to the extent of preventing you from working? Every manager is tired of people making excuses not to work.

The caregiver I just hired, who actually showed up on her first and second day, told me to reduce her pay by several dollars per hour so her income isn't so high that it compromises her food stamps and cash assistance. I have had people tell me they need less-hours so it won't affect their government handouts. This was the first time I have been asked to reduce someone's hourly rate and it is blowing my mind. Then, she ghosted us the next day. No call no show. But this is the kicker; she never filled out the direct deposit paperwork and she hasn't even called to ask for her 16-hour paycheck.

We post help wanted ads for caregivers and receive dozens if not 100 applications. But most applicants don't show up to the interview. Or if they show up, they don't come on their first day. If they do come for orientation, they usually call off repeatedly or never show up again. This is my first-hand consistent experience in the states of Oregon, Nevada, and Arizona. I didn't do the hiring in Texas so I can't say if the problem is just as bad there.

A friend of a current caregiver will work for cash under the table just to fill a shift here and there when we're desperate for a warm body. She doesn't want an actual job because she doesn't want it to affect her disability income. She's on disability because her back hurts ... just like my back hurts, and just my working caregivers whose backs are hurting, too. Yet she won't get a job because she doesn't want to work. There are stage 4 cancer patients and paraplegics out here working. Right now, she and others like her that are milking the system are likely sitting on their butts...watching television...gaining weight...living off tax-payers....feeding disease to potentially become assisted living residents on Medicaid in the next decade or so. This is what our nation has come to. Welfare is no longer a helping hand to get people on their feet. It is life-long income and what people rely on to pay bills and eat.

One of the caregivers that actually shows up most of the time, although she always leaves early and requests time off, is really smart and would be a fantastic employee if her attitude would improve. She smiles, but her energy is burnt out and pissed-off. She doesn't want to work in assisted living, and everyone knows it. She complains to other caregivers and to the families that the nurse doesn't know what she's talking about or she doesn't know how to do her job instead of trying to be on our side. Having conversations with her and writing her up makes no change in her poor attitude so it's time for her to leave. But who will replace her since no one wants to work? I love how my favorite nurse used to refer to caregivers that behave like they are still school children: "They're like glow sticks. You just wanna break em' and shake em' until the light turns on."

Around 100 years ago people were desperate to have a job during and after the Great Depression. Now people aren't working, don't care to work and government handouts are making them nice and cozy at home. Post pandemic, there are way too many companies hiring for people to simply fill out applications, but not work, to continue receiving unemployment. Able bodied workers prefer to sit at home, or they're homeless strung-out on drugs because they're so checked out that they just don't care anymore. The mental health problems in our country are off the charts and it doesn't seem to be improving even though behavioral health companies are springing up across the nation. Our children are mentally unstable, our adults are stressed and depressed, and our thrown-away seniors are skipping meals and meds because they can't afford not to. The anticipation of dementia increasing over 200% likely hasn't factored in the chemically induced dementia cases from pharmaceutical and street drug abuse.

It's my one-year anniversary managing this nice dementia care facility and we still have problems because of inadequate staffing. In my heart, I cannot allow one caregiver to work alone, or have no employees in the building to care for the residents. So, I continue filling shifts for call-off caregivers. Superbowl weekend - On Saturday I got a call off for the morning shift 6AM-2PM. I couldn't find anyone to fill the shift so worked it. Then I had to continue working until 2PM the following day because I got an afternoon call-off, an overnight call-off, and the next morning on Superbowl Sunday I got another call-off. I worked from 6AM on Saturday until 2PM on Sunday. And this is not the first time. How many hours in a row can a human work before crashing and burning out?

The PBS documentary highlighting disaster, which is also available in an audio book version, replays in my mind over and over as I admit high-acuity residents that can't recognize danger while we don't have reliable staff that aren't simply warm bodies. We already have multiple people confused with dementia, sundowning and wandering around all night along, getting into everything. They're falling due to forgetting their walkers or poor balance or trying to ambulate from wheelchairs with no strength left in their legs. One resident has terrible anxiety. She's constantly freaking out thinking someone is after her and she has total body-shakes as she cries uncontrollably. For her it's not sundowning because she's panicked and delusional from morning throughout the night. We have multiple heavy-wetting residents that are bedbound and constantly pressing on their call-buttons. Or worse forgetting to press their buttons for help and being found in odd places.

Four decades ago, assisted living was created to be for people in need of ADL assistance that didn't require a nursing home. And here we are today with epidemics of debilitating diseases and dementia plaguing our nation and assisted living facilities popping up everywhere. People searching for assisted living used to be elders in need of help with toileting and bathing. Yet it's morphing into both young and old with serious medical needs. If we have a building full of high-acuity residents then we will need to raise the already expensive monthly rates to compensate around the clock nurses, highly skilled caregivers, and potentially social workers, and medical directors.

'Build it and they will come'. Well, yes, there are lots of fancy new places and no shortage of people needing care. Marketers and executive directors must have new admissions because people keep dying and more folks are being diagnosed. The dementia piece is so big that it's a book all on its own that I anticipate releasing in the coming year. The mountain of debris being swept under the carpet is hidden behind smiles on social media pages and 'Now Touring' signs. It's a running joke in movies, "Grandpa was admitted into Shady Acres Nursing Home" or whatever. But no one is talking about the excessive lawsuits, the shortage of caregivers, the lack of integrity and scruples at the hands of providers and families... and the fact that one-day sooner than we think you and I will very likely have a stay in a hospital or skilled nursing facility for rehabilitation.

Those of us working in it, those of us who see it every day, may not admit it but most don't want to live in the assisted livings that we're selling. If we don't have boatloads of money or a great private long-term-care insurance policy that covers a massive daily rate, ($100 per day in 2010, $200 per day in 2020, you do the inflation math for the future) then state subsidies for care in a challenged facility will be our lot...unless we put our minds together before then to reconstruct senior care for the future day and age. The discussion on how to improve and move forward must be at the forefront of everyone's minds because in movies we joke about our distressing senior living problem which calls for legislation changes to government hand-outs and facility licensing. We need innovative minds to fix this free-falling private-multi-billion-dollar industry that currently allows seniors in poor neighborhoods to live in squalor while their families complain to executive directors whose hands are tied.

Who should be held accountable for what is being allowed at facilities like Heaven Forbid Senior Living? Acquisition after bad-decision acquisition, highly paid corporate executives make their fortunes and add to their portfolios no matter how badly a facility is functioning. Resources are sent in to rehabilitate worst case scenarios taking away from other locations and burning out once optimistic employees. Even people who want overtime can't function properly when they're working 100 hours per week pulling double shifts every day. And 'too bad' for those of us on salary instead of hourly because we don't get time and a half.

Is accreditation better than state health departments to ensure minimum compliance and care requirements are met? Certainly, the senior living rules and laws of my great-grandparents aren't relevant or efficient for this new common era. I vote to do something quickly because my over-the-hill celebration came and went a long time ago.

104

———◆———

"You're always waiting for a call off. I can't do anything unless it's an hour away. It's always in the back of your mind and it does wear on you. I'm always on, always on my email, on my phone, as the executive director I oversee the building. At least 3 times a month I must go in at night for something."

I'm not the only manager feeling frustrated and concerned for the future, and assisted living isn't the only branch of health care that is suffering from lack of personnel and unethical people coming and going. I received another 'Grand Opening' invitation for a new facility whose corporate executives are very much aware that we already don't have enough caregivers. But that doesn't stop them from building their portfolios and turning their eyes to injustices. If the marketer doesn't produce X amount of move ins this month, I will have to fire her even though we already don't have enough reliable caregivers so my nurse and I must fill shifts … as if we have extra time to do sales, caregiving, and our jobs, too. We don't even have enough cooks in the kitchen. How bad will the extreme greed of senior living executives and companies get? Are there any executives with scruples left in our country of capitalism?

Where do we draw the line to protect our residents with dementia? When a person is deemed incompetent of making their own decisions, when is it unethical for the spouse to continue having 'conjugal' visits in our memory care units? Is it before or after the person no longer recognizes their spouse and can no longer physically scream 'NO!" She's being raped in the dementia care facility, by her own husband, and there's nothing anyone can do about it?? And, she's not the only one.

Speaking of screaming, how can we quickly educate families and residents that screaming at the staff, dropping the F-bomb and nit-picking about every little imperfection within the facility is not helping to be part of the solution? Some important things I would like to get across to people who may read this book is this; "If your mom or dad or grandparent lives to be 90 or 100 years old, the time to worry about them gaining a few extra pounds from eating desserts twice a day is long past. Let them savor the last moments of their lives. Most people in our country don't deny themselves delicious foods, and the sweet taste bud tends to be the last to go so why not allow elders their final pleasures? Why must we wake up residents at 6:00 AM to get them dressed and in the dining room by 8:00 AM if they would prefer to sleep in?

Just as with children many seniors don't want to eat their vegetables or simply can't stomach healthy foods after decades of eating processed foods. It's not time to worry about them gaining a few pounds. I'm more worried about them losing weight. With only a few years left of life, shouldn't they have their 100th birthday cake and be allowed to eat it too? Some families really want the best for their loved ones but have a hard time letting go so they try every which way to keep them alive even when the person just wants to be left in peace. I constantly see my residents cave into their family's wishes even though they can't breathe, are in terrible pain, and it's not what the resident wants. Maybe families should ask and listen instead of dictating and demanding. Just because you're their Power of Attorney (POA) doesn't give you permission to deprive them of making their own decisions and enjoying quality-of-life activities. POA, that paper only goes so far. Yet, even when the POA document isn't in effect meaning the person hasn't been deemed incompetent to make their own decisions, families bully seniors 'out of love'.

We know your loved one means the world to you, and you don't want them to die. Yet, everything that lives must eventually die – every bug, plant, fish, bird, animal, and human will eventually die .... and it's ok. We all go to sleep and that's a normal part of life. But to force more pills and procedures on people who are tired and at the end of their lives is not compassionate. Or forcing more physical therapy on them when they're legs don't work, and they're exhausted just wanting to be left alone, isn't always in the dying person's best interest. They may not be actively transitioning/dying, but they're at the end of their lives. Too many families don't listen to us when we see their loved one needs to be on Hospice pain management. Just because a person goes on Hospice doesn't mean they're going to die right away. It's not a death sentence to be on Hospice. People get booted off Hospice all the time because medically they no longer qualify. But if you really love then then why keep allowing your loved one to suffer? Regular old over-the-counter meds 'as needed' are not going to keep your loved one comfortable if they're in severe pain.

A family came to tour yesterday for their mom who is 83 years old, uses a Hoyer-lift because she can't bear any weight, is incontinent of bladder and bowel, and she has severe dementia. "Our budget is $6000 per month because we need to make sure her money lasts for at least five years." I couldn't say what I was thinking because I am not God and cannot see the future. However, in my almost 20 years of experience with dementia I know her mom will likely die in around 2 years, possibly even less. But I can't say that. And many doctors won't say it either because we don't want families to get upset.

One resident's family doesn't want their 87-year-old mom to go on Hospice, but she screams when we barely even touch her. It is so distressing for us to see her in so much pain, for her to scream bloody-murder at the slightest touch. Another family doesn't want their 90+ year old mom to go onto Hospice and she is literally staring into space, disconnected from reality and in the last stage of dementia. Too many families are in denial thinking that their loved one is going to get better when they are at the end of their life. In her living will it states that she doesn't want her life prolonged but her adult children don't care what their mom wants. We understand you love your mom or dad or grandparent or spouse (or whoever they are to you) but they're not going to get better so stop make making them feel guilty.

105

—◆—

"*I feel so bad for one resident because her husband is literally forcing her to walk and do laps around the building, and she is breaking down physically. She hates it when her husband visits because he has her sweating out of breath. He doesn't care how she feels, he just wants her to get better. But she just wants to be left alone. The husband wants large portions to be on her plate, and she can't eat that much so she feels bad that so much food goes to waste. When he eats with her in the dining room he complains about the food and tries to get the other residents to start complaining even though the food is good and everyone else likes it. And he's always changing her medications, so the nurse is always having to enter new doctor's orders. He passive-aggressively bullies and belittles and talks crap about everyone. All the staff hate it when he comes in the building.*"

With all the Baby boomers filtering into assisted living facilities it's time to start contemplating what we want for ourselves instead of allowing our children or the courts to decide for us. If facilities keep popping up at the current rate, then those facilities are being built for you and me knowing none of us will live forever. But who will be there to care for us? Our adult children will be at work trying to make ends meet and they won't have the time, energy, or patience to physically take care of us. I mean, let's face it, we no longer have three and four generations living in the same home.

Once upon a time we were born and died in the home but now we are born and die in medical institutions, you know the same ones that are understaffed. Americans are removed from death making us even more fearful of the inevitable thus prolonging life for as long as possible. How is Medicare and Medicaid going to support our aging population when most of our taxes go to war instead of helping the people in our nation? Yeah, I said it. What about us in America? Are we citizens of the greatest nation on earth or civilians trying to survive in the filthy war of diseases while we clean up other countries? If we can send billions of dollars at a time, month after month, year after year, decade after decade, to provide weapons and get involved in other countries drama, then why can't we clean up our own house? If trillions of dollars can evaporate into thin air from our national defense fund, then why can't we spend a few billion to prevent illnesses from our country's rusted water pipes and decaying 20th century infrastructure? We can't even drink our own tap water. Our healthcare system is collapsing before our eyes and we still re-elect the same wealthy politicians, century after century. The rich can afford quality care, but what about the rest of us?

As I wrap up this book, I just received a phone call from an attorney about a potential lawsuit regarding the resident that died from the broken neck incident at Heaven Forbid. This is an uncomfortable feeling. I do not want to be called into arbitration. One of my colleagues almost had a nervous breakdown after having to testify in a different case last week. I conducted training after training with the staff in that facility as with every facility I have managed. But the caregivers simply didn't care, and they put the lady back in bed after she fell and sustained a broken neck. How much training can one lead to convince caregivers to pay attention and dial 911? Assisted living facilities are relying on 'no-show' cold hearted warm bodies to be caregivers for debilitated Americans.

I became an executive director because I am strong in operations. Now I am learning how to work with feeding tubes, catheters, and ostomies because people don't want to work, and the only inquiries for new residents coming in are for seniors that are in their final weeks, days, even hours of life. Where do we draw the 'scope of practice' line? Are we nursing homes now? We're barely keeping it together as assisted livings so how are the rehabilitation facilities, hospitals, and nursing homes coping in this senior tsunami without adequate staff?

For the love of all things that are still good on earth, please...will the next scheduled caregiver show up to work without requiring a bonus on top of hourly pay? How did we go from catching two buses just to get to work on time, to demanding cash incentives from our bosses to fill our normally scheduled shifts? Can you imagine calling your boss and saying, "I will come to work if you give me a $100 gas card because my tank is empty." Or worse yet, imagine your only option is to live in a 'worst case scenario' Medicaid facility of bugs, thugs, and drugs.

THE END

About the Author

Unable to help as two of her grandparents slipped away with Parkinson's and Alzheimer's dementia, Jen felt hopeless when she discovered there was little reprieve for those living with it. After her grandfather was sent to a skilled nursing facility, she was heartbroken when the nurses commented, "He doesn't know what you're doing anyway," as if he was deaf, too. When Jen learned about the attitudes in the facility, she became disheartened with the lack of compassion on the WW2 veteran's last birthday.

Working as an activity director at an assisted living and dementia care community in 2006, Jen encouraged residents in wheelchairs with little to no communication skills to participate in balloon volleyball, work puzzles, and sing songs from their era. Although there was little training for her to understand the clinical diagnoses of the people she was helping, she knew that they had pasts that were rich, and that each one mattered just like her grandparents. Jen began taking classes and reached out to others in her field to find out what methods they used to create activities within their buildings. Working with countless residents, activity directors, marketers, caregivers, nurses, chefs, executive directors, neurologists, and dementia specialists, Jen began to understand and experience the many dimensions of dementia. She began implementing daily intergenerational programs and writing books offering fun activity ideas to do with people in all stages of the disease process.

In 2011, Jen was hired to assist with activities for a dementia care company in Arizona. She noted that there was no training program for these positions and once again she relied on her own curious nature. Her success was noticed by the corporate directors, and she was transferred to a nearby sister-community to develop their activity program. A couple of years later Jen transitioned to business office manager and this job exposed her to a new area of the industry. She was encouraged to advance her career in Senior Living and take the next step in managing a community.

Earning her managers license in 2013 and taking on the role of executive director, she began to enjoy making the changes she deemed necessary to help her staff and residents. Jen's responsibilities increased when she moved up the corporate ladder into regional operations roles training new executive directors, marketers, activity directors and dietary managers in different states. Her path took her into in-home care companies where she saw the inner workings of staffing agencies that she once called upon to fill open shifts in facilities.

At times, Jen vowed to walk away from this broken system, only to be talked into helping a community or a friend in the business who traveled the same road she was on. For Jen, this went on for years as she wandered in a healthcare system that at the best of times seemed broken and the worst of times, left her with sleepless nights and threatened her own health. Assisted Living Manager, Dementia Practitioner, and End-of-Life Doula, from Independent Living to Assisted Living and Dementia-Care, from Texas, to Nevada, to Oregon, Jen has transversed the senior care industry. **An author since childhood, a public speaker and guest speaker on radio and television, and an online video content creator,** Jen remains positive and hopeful that we will put our minds together and build the next paradigm in senior care.

Made in United States
North Haven, CT
06 May 2023

36311839R00108